JAMES MARTIN

masterclass

JAMES MARTIN

masterclass

MAKE YOUR HOME COOKING EASIER

Collins

First published in 2011 by Collins
an imprint of HarperCollins*Publishers*
77–85 Fulham Palace Road
London W6 8JB

www.harpercollins.co.uk

10 9 8 7 6 5 4 3 2 1

Photography © Peter Cassidy 2011
Text © James Martin 2011
Publishing Director: Jenny Heller
Editorial: Ione Walder
Food styling: Linda Tubby
Prop styling: Sue Rowlands
Many thanks to David Mellor Design for their generous loan of cutlery and props.

James Martin asserts his moral right to be identified as the author of this work.

A catalogue record for this book is available from the British Library.

ISBN: 978-0-00-729472-5

Colour reproduction by Saxon Digital, printed and bound by Butler Tanner and Dennis Ltd.

CONTENTS

INTRODUCTION

There are certain cookery skills that form the basis of all dishes. These basic skills, combined with good ingredients and the application of heat are all that is needed to achieve great cooking. Take a soufflé, for example. You can spend hours whisking egg whites and buttering the dishes, but if your basic white sauce is wrong the dish just won't succeed. However, with current food trends changing at such a pace and chefs constantly trying to reinvent the wheel, these essential kitchen skills can sometimes get overlooked.

If there is one thing I've learnt from my time presenting *Saturday Kitchen*, it's that we should never stop listening or learning. While this means being open to exciting new techniques and methods, it also means taking the time to step backwards and perfect the basics, to get the essential skills right, because these underpin everything else you cook. Letting other people share their knowledge and wisdom with you is also key to becoming a better cook. I've had the honour and privilege of meeting many brilliant chefs, from Daniel Boulud, with his three Michelin stars, to my true friend Michel Roux Senior, one of the world's greatest chefs. Working alongside people like this, you quickly get an insight into what is happening in the world of food, and they have taught me a lot. And perhaps the ultimate compliment is when a great chef has learnt something from *me*: for example, if they place one of my dishes on their menu. (As a result, I now have Michel Roux's restaurant menu up on the wall in my loo, but please don't tell him!) It just goes to show that, no matter how old or accomplished you are, there is always something more you can learn.

So with this in mind, I've considered the many skills, techniques and bits of knowledge that I've picked up throughout my career and have gathered the best of them together for you in this book. Inside these covers you will find the very basics, including step-by-step instructions for filleting fish, jointing chicken and mastering that classic white sauce. I also share the best recipes and nuggets of information that I've absorbed during my travels around the world, including a recipe for the most delicious pasta sauce that I tasted in Naples and some amazing grissini sticks that I ate in Venice, whilst others stay true to my love for British food, such as Arbroath smokies (my food heaven) blended into a pâté and served with warm toasts.

Over the last decade, I've watched the food and ingredients we use in this country change a lot, with specialist and exotic ingredients now much more readily available. I've also learnt that it's amazing to find what is right on your doorstep when you go out and look for it, with some really excellent local produce available to us. Sadly, many local producers and farmers are going out of business, due to a lack of knowledge about their ingredients, as well as the importation of cheap foreign food. I firmly believe that there is no such thing as food that is cheap and good. You get for what you pay for. That's not to say it needs to be stupidly expensive, but British beef is worth the extra cost because it tastes brilliant, and the same goes for seasonal strawberries and fresh seafood; these are the luxuries of living where we do. So not only should we be reinforcing our basic cooking skills, we should also be looking after our suppliers and producers by giving them our custom – because once they are gone, the void will be a long time filled and our cooking won't be as successful.

Learning from the experience of other people is perhaps the best way to become a better cook, so I hope that *Masterclass* will equip you with the essential kitchen skills, and give you more confidence in the kitchen. To all the chefs and foodie people who have taught me something along the way, thank you, and to those who I will meet in the future, I look forward to tasting your food and listening to your stories.

James

CHAPTER 1
SOUPS, STEWS & PIES

CREAM OF CAULIFLOWER SOUP

The texture of this soup is so velvety; it can be eaten simply as a snack but is also elegant enough for a dinner party. If you want to make it even more sophisticated, you can serve it with seared scallops. The use of curry powder with cauliflower certainly isn't a new combination – it helps to offset the soup's richness. The most important thing with this soup, however, is the cooking. You wouldn't overcook cauliflower normally, so don't do it when it's in a soup.

SERVES 4
VEGETARIAN

30g (1¼oz) butter

1 clove of garlic, peeled and crushed

½ white onion, peeled and diced

225g (8oz) potatoes, peeled and diced

½ tsp mild curry powder

75ml (3fl oz) white wine

750ml (1 pint 6fl oz) vegetable stock

1 large cauliflower, cut into florets

100g (3½oz) diced leek (white part only)

2 slices of white bread (crusts removed), cut into cubes

2 tbsp extra-virgin olive oil, plus extra for drizzling

200ml (7fl oz) double cream

Salt and black pepper

1. Melt the butter in a large, heavy-based saucepan over a medium heat and when it starts to foam, add the garlic and onion and fry, without browning, for 2–3 minutes.

2. Add the potatoes, curry powder, white wine and stock and bring to the boil, then reduce the heat and simmer for 5 minutes or until the potatoes are tender. Add the cauliflower and leek and simmer for a further 6–8 minutes or until the cauliflower is just cooked.

3. Meanwhile, place a small frying pan over a high heat and sauté the bread in the olive oil for 2–3 minutes or until browned, then drain on kitchen paper and set aside.

4. Pour the cream into the saucepan and bring back up to the boil, then remove from the heat and allow to cool for 2–3 minutes. Transfer the contents of the pan to a food processor or blender and purée until smooth. Pour the soup back into the pan and gently bring to a simmer, then season with salt and pepper.

5. Divide between bowls, then sprinkle with the croûtons, drizzle with olive oil and serve immediately.

LEEK AND ROCKET SOUP WITH GOAT'S CHEESE

This classic combination of flavours is a favourite of many. It's important to pay close attention to the cooking time because if you cook the soup for too long you will lose the flavours and the colour. This soup is also good served cold, but it may be a good idea to add a little more liquid, as the texture tends to change and thicken as it cools. I like to use Mrs Wecksby's goat's cheese, or Perroche goat's cheese from Neal's Yard, but any other soft goat's cheese will do fine too.

SERVES 4
VEGETARIAN

1–2 tbsp olive oil

1 large potato, peeled and cut into small dice

1 white onion, peeled and roughly chopped

1 sprig of thyme

2 leeks, trimmed and chopped

1 litre (1¾ pints) vegetable stock

150ml (5fl oz) double cream

100g (3½oz) rocket leaves

Salt and black pepper

TO SERVE
200g (7oz) soft goat's cheese
1 sprig of chervil, chopped

1. Place a heavy-based pan over a medium heat, pour in the olive oil and add the potato, onion and thyme, then sauté, without browning, for 2–3 minutes. Add the leeks and cook for 1 further minute. Pour in the stock and bring to the boil, then reduce the heat and simmer for about 10 minutes.

2. Pour in the cream and bring back up to the boil, then remove from the heat and allow to cool slightly. Pour the soup into a blender and pulse until smooth, then add the rocket leaves and pulse again. Transfer the soup back into the pan and gently bring to a simmer, then season with salt and pepper.

3. Divide the soup between bowls, crumble over the goat's cheese, garnish with the chervil and serve.

PISTOU SOUP

A great classic soup with pesto added right at the end, this is easy to make and nice as a starter or a simple snack. It's definitely a summer soup and you should always use the very best fresh summer vegetables to give maximum colour and flavour. I mix and match the pasta, as it's a good way to use up broken or leftover bits. The best pistou soup I have come across was in Nice. Not surprising when you consider that the ingredients in its famous Niçoise salad are pretty similar to the ingredients for pistou.

SERVES 6–8

11 plum tomatoes

100g (3½oz) frozen broad beans

4 tbsp olive oil

1 onion, peeled and chopped

2 cloves of garlic, peeled and chopped

1 leek, trimmed and diced

2 carrots, peeled and diced

2 courgettes, topped, tailed and diced

2 potatoes, peeled and diced

1 x 250g can of haricot beans, drained and rinsed

75g (3oz) dried spaghetti

75g (3oz) French beans, topped and tailed and cut into 4 pieces

100g (3½oz) frozen peas

Salt and black pepper

1 handful of basil leaves, to garnish

FOR THE PISTOU

60g (2½oz) fresh basil leaves

4 cloves of garlic, peeled

1 skinned, deseeded and chopped tomato (reserved from step 5)

75g (3oz) grated Parmesan cheese

135ml (4½fl oz) extra-virgin olive oil

1. Score a cross in the bottom of each tomato, place in a bowl and cover with boiling water. Leave for 45 seconds, then drain and peel off the skin. Cut the tomatoes into quarters, remove the seeds and chop the flesh. Blanch the broad beans for 2–3 minutes in boiling water, then refresh in cold water and peel off the skins.

2. Place a large, heavy-based saucepan over a medium heat, add the olive oil and all the chopped and diced vegetables except the tomatoes and fry, without browning, for 4–5 minutes.

3. Add the haricot beans, fill with enough water to cover, and bring to the boil.

4. Meanwhile, wrap the spaghetti in a clean tea towel and crush it on the edge of a worktop, pressing it backwards and forwards to break it into small pieces, then add these to the soup.

5. Add all but one of the chopped tomatoes (reserving this last one for the pistou), bring back up to the boil, reduce the heat and simmer for 15 minutes or until the pasta is cooked. After 10–11 minutes, add the French beans, broad beans and peas. (It's best to add these at the end of cooking in order to preserve their fresh colour.)

6. While the soup is cooking, place all the pistou ingredients in a blender and purée to a paste.

7. Remove the soup from the heat and stir in the pistou. Season well with salt and pepper and serve straight away.

CREAM OF TOMATO SOUP WITH ROASTED VINE TOMATOES

It was tomatoes that got me interested in food in the first place; as a kid, the smell of them growing in my grandad's greenhouse intoxicated me. I still love them so much and the first thing I did when I last moved house was to build my own greenhouse in which to grow them. Every time I open the door the smell sends me back 30 years. For this soup, the tomatoes must be the best you can get, and vine tomatoes are ideal because they are usually the freshest.

SERVES 4
VEGETARIAN

1.5kg (3lb 4oz) vine tomatoes

100g (3½oz) butter

½ large onion,
peeled and chopped

3 cloves of garlic,
peeled and chopped

1 stick of celery,
trimmed and chopped

2 tbsp tomato ketchup

2 tbsp tomato purée

1 sprig of thyme

200ml (7fl oz) double cream,
plus extra to serve (optional)

Salt and black pepper

FOR THE ROASTED VINE TOMATOES
4 bunches of 3–4 small vine tomatoes

2–3 tbsp olive oil

1 tbsp balsamic vinegar

1. Preheat the oven to 200°C (400°F), Gas 6.

2. Remove the 1.5kg (3lb 4oz) of tomatoes from the vines and chop each tomato into 6, keeping the vines.

3. Melt half the butter in a large, heavy-based saucepan over a medium heat, then add the onion, tomatoes, garlic and celery. Add the ketchup and tomato purée, cover with a lid and bring to the boil.

4. Strip the thyme leaves from the stalks and add the leaves to the pan, reduce the heat to a simmer, then place the vines from the tomatoes on the top, cover with the lid and simmer for 15 minutes. (Be careful not to let it boil, as the vegetables may catch on the bottom of the pan.)

5. Meanwhile, place the 4 bunches of small vine tomatoes (keeping them on the vines) on a baking tray, drizzle with the olive oil and the vinegar, season with salt and pepper and roast in the oven for 5–6 minutes or until softened.

6. Remove the lid from the saucepan, discard the vines and pour in the cream. Remove from the heat, transfer to a blender and pulse until smooth, then pass though a sieve to remove the tomato seeds. Pour the soup back into the pan and reheat gently, trying not to let it boil, then season well with salt and pepper.

7. Serve the soup with a bunch of roasted vine tomatoes in the bottom of each bowl and, if you like, a spoonful of cream swirled on top of the soup.

MUSHROOM SOUP WITH CORIANDER CRESS

I remember going mushroom picking in the New Forest when I was a junior chef. The head chef said it was an inspiring exercise – looking back now, I can see his point, but I also reckon it was cheap forced labour! Fast forward 20 years however, and I'm still doing it. Most recently I went with Nick Nairn up in Scotland. Rowing across the loch on our way to find mushrooms, neither of us exactly looked like Captain Jack Sparrow, but the treasure we came back with was much better than pirate gold – delicious fresh wild mushrooms with a great intense flavour.

SERVES 4

1kg (2lb 3oz) field mushrooms

100ml (3½fl oz) rapeseed oil

2 large shallots, peeled and chopped

2 cloves of garlic, peeled and chopped

Juice of ½ lemon

500ml (18fl oz) chicken stock (see pages 64–5)

250ml (9fl oz) double cream

125g (4½oz) butter, diced

250g (9oz) mixed wild mushrooms (such as chanterelle, cep, trompette, girolle or oyster)

5g (¼oz) chervil, chopped

50g (2oz) coriander cress or micro salad leaves

Salt and black pepper

1. Remove the stalks from the field mushrooms and, using a spoon, scrape away and discard the dark gills, then cut the mushrooms into slices about 5mm (¼in) thick.

2. Place a large, heavy-based saucepan over a medium heat, pour in half the rapeseed oil, then add the shallots and garlic and cook for 1–2 minutes or until softened. Add the sliced mushrooms, season with salt and pepper, and cook for 3–4 minutes.

3. Stir in the lemon juice then pour in the stock, bring to the boil, reduce the heat and simmer gently for 10 minutes.

4. Transfer the contents of the pan into a blender and whizz to a smooth purée – this should take a good 2–3 minutes. Pour back into the pan, add the cream and mix thoroughly. Gently warm over a low heat, then stir in the diced butter, adjust the seasoning, if needed, and keep warm on the hob.

5. Pour the remainder of the oil into a frying pan over a medium heat and sauté the mixed wild mushrooms for about 3 minutes or until cooked through, then season and set aside.

6. To serve, divide the cooked wild mushrooms between bowls, ladle over the soup and sprinkle with the chervil and coriander cress or micro salad leaves.

CULLEN SKINK

This Scottish soup from the town of Cullen in Moray is one of those great classic soups, with most of its flavour provided by the main ingredient – smoked haddock. Traditionally, it should be made with Finnan Haddie, which is smoked haddock from Findon near Aberdeen, but any other natural smoked haddock will do.

SERVES 4

2 Arbroath Smokies

75g (3oz) unsalted butter

2 banana shallots, peeled and finely chopped

100g (3½oz) diced leek (white part only)

2 cloves of garlic, peeled and finely chopped

200g (7oz) waxy boiled potatoes, peeled

1 litre (1¾ pints) fish stock

100ml (3½fl oz) white wine

200ml (7fl oz) milk

125ml (4½fl oz) double cream

Black pepper

2 tsp chopped chives, to garnish

1. Remove the skin and bones from the fish and flake the flesh.

2. Melt a third of the butter in a large, heavy-based saucepan over a medium heat, then add the shallots, leek and garlic. Cover the pan with a lid and sweat, without browning, for 5–10 minutes.

3. Cut the potatoes into 2cm (¾in) dice and add to the vegetables, together with three-quarters of the flaked fish (reserving the remaining quarter for later). Cover again with the lid and cook for a further 2 minutes, then pour in the stock and wine. Bring to the boil, then reduce the heat and simmer for 8 minutes.

4. Remove from the heat and allow to cool slightly before carefully transferring the mixture to a blender. Whizz for a few seconds, then add the milk and cream, a little at a time, and blend for 4–5 minutes or until the mixture is very smooth, then pass through a sieve into a clean pan.

5. Gently reheat then add the remaining fish and butter and season well with pepper. Divide between bowls, scatter over the chopped chives and serve with some warm crusty bread.

BEEF MADRAS CURRY

I think India should be on everybody's list of places to visit, to experience the amazing range of foods and the many different people who live there. This curry takes its name from the city of Madras, in the south of India. It can be made with most meats or it can also be vegetarian. As with most Indian dishes, there were many variations but this was my favourite, from a small café and just served with flatbread. I had the recipe translated into English so that you can enjoy it as much as I did.

SERVES 4–6

800g (1¾lb) stewing beef, cut into 2.5cm (1in) dice

4–5 tbsp vegetable oil

1 green chilli, deseeded and chopped

1 clove of garlic, peeled and chopped

2cm (¾in) piece of root ginger, peeled and chopped

1 onion, peeled and finely sliced

12 curry leaves

3 cardamon pods, crushed

2 bay leaves

1 x 400g can of chopped tomatoes

200ml (7fl oz) beef stock

3 tbsp tamarind paste

25g (1oz) butter

25g (1oz) flat-leaf parsley, chopped

Salt and black pepper

1. For the madras curry powder, place all of the whole spices in a spice grinder or coffee grinder, or use a pestle and mortar, and grind to a fine powder, then mix with the ground turmeric and vegetable oil.

2. Next, season the beef all over with salt and pepper. Heat 1–2 tablespoons of the vegetable oil in a large, non-stick saucepan and, over a high heat, sear roughly a third or a half of the beef pieces for 1–2 minutes or until golden brown. Fry the rest of the beef in 1–2 more batches, removing each batch from the pan when the meat is browned and placing it on a plate while you fry the remaining pieces, adding more oil as needed.

3. Blend the chilli, garlic and ginger to a paste using a hand-held blender or a pestle and mortar and adding a splash of water if necessary.

4. Place the pan used to seal the beef back over a high heat, add 1–2 tablespoons of the vegetable oil and the onion and fry for 5 minutes or until softened and starting to brown. Add 3½ tablespoons of the curry powder, along with the chilli, garlic and ginger paste, the curry leaves, cardamom and bay leaves, then stir the mixture well.

Continued...

FOR THE MADRAS CURRY POWDER

2 tbsp coriander seeds

2 tbsp fenugreek seeds

1 tbsp black mustard seeds

1 tsp cumin seeds

½ tsp fennel seeds

1 tsp black peppercorns

1 cinnamon stick

5 cloves

1 tbsp ground turmeric

2 tbsp vegetable oil

FOR THE FRIED SHALLOTS

3 shallots, peeled and finely sliced

2 tbsp plain flour

100ml (3½fl oz) vegetable oil

5. Tip in the beef and cover with the chopped tomatoes, stock and tamarind paste, then season with salt and pepper. Cover the pan with a lid and bring to the boil, then reduce the heat to low and simmer for 2 hours or until the beef is very tender. Alternatively, cook in the oven, preheated to 140C° (275°F), Gas 1, for 2 hours, or in a slow cooker for 3–4 hours.

6. For the fried shallots, first dust the shallots in the flour. Place a frying pan over a high heat, pour in the vegetable oil and fry the shallots for 2–3 minutes or until crisp and golden brown. Remove from the oil and drain on kitchen paper.

7. Remove the lid from the curry pan, stir in the butter and chopped parsley and season to taste. Spoon the beef on to plates with some of the crispy shallots on top and serve with some plain boiled rice on the side.

BEEF BOURGUIGNON

Classic dishes shouldn't be messed about with. Beef bourguignon is one of those classics and this recipe has come via the long road from my training days in France. In between the pints of French *bière* I got a lot of practice at dishes like hake beurre blanc, duck gizzards salads and lemon tarts, and of course this one. It's still exactly the same as it was back then, just as it should be.

SERVES 4

2 tbsp plain flour

1kg (2lb 3oz) braising steak,
cut into 2.5cm (1in) dice

4–5 tbsp olive oil

150g (5oz) pancetta,
cut into small chunks

1 shallot, peeled and finely chopped

2 onions, peeled and sliced

1 garlic clove, peeled and crushed

75ml (3fl oz) brandy

500ml (18fl oz) red wine

1 litre (1¾ pints) beef stock

1 bouquet garni (2 bay leaves,
2 sprigs of thyme, 2 sprigs
of flat-leaf parsley)

115g (4oz) baby onions

25g (1oz) butter

Salt and black pepper

1. Season the flour with salt and pepper and toss the beef in it. Place a large, non-stick frying pan over a high heat, add 1–2 tablespoons of olive oil and fry the beef for 1–2 minutes in batches, removing each batch from the pan when browned and placing it on a plate while you fry the rest, adding more oil as needed. (Too much meat in the pan at once will mean it takes longer to brown.)

2. Add the pancetta and fry for 1–2 minutes or until golden brown, then tip in the shallot, onions and garlic and fry for a further 2–3 minutes or until browned. Return the cooked beef to the pan and mix well with the other ingredients.

3. Pour in the brandy and carefully set it alight to burn off the alcohol, then add the wine and stock and bring to a simmer. Add the bouquet garni, then cover and cook on a low heat for 2 hours or until tender and thickened. Alternatively, cook in the oven at 140°C (275°F), Gas 1, for 2 hours, or in a slow cooker for 3–4 hours.

4. Half an hour before the meat is cooked, blanch the baby onions in boiling water for 30 seconds, then peel. Place a separate frying pan over a high heat, add the butter and a little olive oil and fry the onions for 2–3 minutes or until just golden, then add to the casserole for the last 20 minutes of cooking time.

5. Just before serving, check the seasoning. Spoon a generous portion of beef bourguignon on to each plate and a pile of Creamy Potato Mash (see page 179) alongside, together with some green beans or Vichy Carrots (see page 174).

COURGETTE, TOMATO AND BASIL PIE WITH DORSTONE CHEESE

Dorstone is a cheese I came across once at a farmers' market, made by Charlie Westhead of Neal's Yard Dairy. It's an unpasteurised goat's cheese made in Herefordshire, with a moist, fluffy texture and coated in ash. If you can't get it, don't worry; a non-chalky goat's cheese will do fine, even a French Crottin.

SERVES 4

2–3 tbsp olive oil, plus extra for oiling

4 courgettes, topped and tailed and sliced lengthways

1 x 250g jar of sun-blushed tomatoes, drained

2 banana shallots, peeled and chopped

2 cloves of garlic, peeled

6 large basil leaves, torn

200g (7oz) firm goat's cheese, such as Dorstone or Ogleshield

Plain flour, for dusting

200g (7oz) ready-rolled all-butter puff pastry

1 egg, beaten

Salt and black pepper

ONE 25CM (10IN) OVENPROOF DISH

1. Preheat the oven 170°C (325°F), Gas 3, and oil the ovenproof dish with olive oil.

2. Lay the courgettes on a baking tray, season with salt and pepper and drizzle with the olive oil. Bake in the oven for 10 minutes or until they start to turn golden brown, then remove from the oven and allow to cool.

3. Place the tomatoes, shallots, garlic and basil leaves in a bowl and season with salt and pepper. Add the baked courgettes and mix well, then crumble over the cheese and set aside.

4. On a clean, lightly floured work surface, lay out the pastry and cut out a circle 2cm (¾in) wider all round than the ovenproof dish. Place the courgette mix in the dish, then brush the edges of the dish with some of the beaten egg and lay the pastry on top, pressing the edges of the pastry on to the rim of the dish. Trim away any excess pastry and brush the top of the pie with the remaining egg.

5. Bake in the oven for about 20 minutes or until the pastry is golden brown, then remove and serve immediately.

JAMES'S SHEPHERD'S PIE

Who says British food isn't great? I keep saying to people and young chefs that the best way to move forward in terms of cooking is often to look back. Shepherd's Pie with garden peas is a dinner my mother used to cook all the time and still does. Look out for minced lamb that isn't fatty as this will make it much better. And don't put too much liquid in the mash or it will be too soft and the potatoes will just sink into the meat mixture.

SERVES 4

1–2 tbsp olive oil

1.5kg (3lb 4oz) boneless
shoulder of lamb

300g (11oz) baby onions, blanched
and peeled (see method on page 20)

2 cloves of garlic, peeled
and finely chopped

4 sprigs of rosemary

500ml (18fl oz) red wine

500ml (18fl oz) beef stock

75g (3oz) butter

25g (1oz) plain flour

Salt and black pepper

FOR THE MASH TOPPING

500g (1lb 2oz) large floury potatoes,
such as King Edward, peeled
and cut into quarters

50g (2oz) butter

100ml (3½fl oz) whole milk

1. Preheat the oven to 200°C (400°F), Gas 6. Heat the olive oil in a large casserole dish, season the lamb with salt and pepper on both sides, then seal the meat all over on a high heat for 1–2 minutes or until nicely browned.

2. Remove the lamb from the pot and add the baby onions, frying these for 2–3 minutes or until golden, then add the garlic and 3 sprigs of rosemary.

3. Place the lamb back in the pot on top of the onions and rosemary, then pour in the wine and stock. Smear a third of the butter over the lamb and place the remaining rosemary sprig on top. Roast in the oven, uncovered, for 2 hours or until tender and crispy on top.

4. Meanwhile, make the mashed potato for the topping following the instructions for Creamy Potato Mash on page 179.

5. When the lamb is cooked, remove from the pot and strain the juices into a small saucepan set over a medium heat, keeping the onions for later. Mix the flour and remaining butter together to form a paste, then break into pieces and add to the juices in the pan, whisking until you have a thick gravy. Tear the meat into large chunks and place in the ovenproof dish. Add the reserved onions and pour over the thickened juices.

6. Put the mashed potato into a piping bag and pipe or spoon it over the meat and spread evenly with a fork. Bake in the oven for 25 minutes or until the top is golden brown. Serve with purple sprouting broccoli and Vichy Carrots (see page 174).

CHICKEN AND WILD MUSHROOM PIE

You can make this chicken pie either with brown or white meat or a combination of both. The same goes for the mushrooms – use either fresh or dried or whatever you can get hold of. Porcini, ceps and morels are the classics to put with chicken, or for something different you could replace them with water chestnuts. Fresh tarragon is much better than dried for this recipe, but do remember that it's a strongly flavoured herb, so don't add too much.

SERVES 6–8

375g (13oz) ready-rolled all-butter puff pastry

1 egg, beaten

FOR THE FILLING

1 x 1.5kg (3lb 4oz) chicken

2 onions, peeled and finely chopped

1 bay leaf

1 tbsp olive oil

75g (3oz) butter

2 tbsp plain flour

350g (12oz) wild mushrooms (such as chanterelle, cep, trompette, girolle or oyster)

150ml (5fl oz) white wine

150ml (5fl oz) double cream

4 sprigs of tarragon, leaves only

Salt and black pepper

ONE 20 X 30CM (8 X 12IN) PIE DISH OR OVENPROOF DISH

1. Place the chicken in a large saucepan with half the onions and the bay leaf. Season with a little salt and pepper and cover with water. Bring to the boil, then reduce the heat and simmer for 45 minutes or until the chicken is cooked through.

2. Remove the chicken from the pan and set aside to cool. Return the pan to the hob and cook the stock on a rapid boil for a further 30 minutes or until it has reduced by half. Meanwhile, remove the meat from the chicken legs, thighs and carcass, then place in the pie dish.

3. Preheat the oven to 220°C (425°F), Gas 7. Heat the olive oil and butter in a large frying pan, add the remaining onions and cook over a low–medium heat, without browning, for about 5 minutes or until softened, then add the flour. Turn up the heat then add the mushrooms and cook for a further 3–4 minutes.

4. Strain the stock, then add to the mushrooms and cook for 1 minute. Pour in the wine and cream, then bring to the boil, reduce the heat and simmer for 5 minutes. Season, then pour it over the chicken and sprinkle tarragon leaves over the top.

5. Cut out a disc of pastry 2cm (¾in) wider all round than the pie dish. Brush the edges of the dish with beaten egg and lay the pastry on top, crimping the edges with a fork or your fingertips. Trim away any excess pastry and brush the top of the pie with the remaining egg. Place on a baking tray and bake for 30–35 minutes or until the pastry is crisp and golden. Then remove from the oven and allow to cool slightly before serving with new potatoes and French beans.

BEEF SHIN AND CARROT PIES

This pie is best made with Hereford beef, a breed that originated in the UK but is now farmed everywhere from Russia to South America. The cows have a deep red coat and fantastic horns, and their meat is highly prized. We use Hereford beef in the restaurant for our steaks, as the meat has an excellent grain. If you can't find it, any breed will do, as it's the long slow cooking that really gives this pie its flavour – the longer you cook it for, the better it will taste. I suggest serving the pie with French beans or shallots.

SERVES 4

800g (1¾lb) trimmed beef shin or flank, cut into 3cm (1¼in) dice

2 tbsp plain flour

4–5 tbsp olive oil

30g (1¼oz) butter

1 onion, peeled and finely chopped

1 clove of garlic, peeled and crushed

1 tbsp tomato purée

200ml (7fl oz) Guinness

500ml (18fl oz) beef stock

1 tsp chopped thyme leaves

1 bay leaf

300g (11oz) small Chantenay carrots, trimmed and kept whole

Salt and black pepper

FOR THE PASTRY

225g (8oz) self-raising flour, sifted, plus extra for dusting

1 tsp salt

90g (3¼oz) shredded beef suet

60g (2½oz) lard or butter, chilled and grated

1 egg, beaten

FOUR 500ML (18FL OZ) PIE DISHES

1. Preheat the oven to 200°C (400°F), Gas 6. Lightly dust the meat with flour, salt and pepper. Heat 1–2 tablespoons of olive oil in a large, heavy-based frying pan or saucepan, add the meat in batches, using more of the oil if needed, and seal over a high heat for 1–2 minutes or until nicely browned. Transfer to a plate and set aside.

2. Melt the butter in the pan, add the onion and garlic and fry for 2–3 minutes or until browned, then stir in the tomato purée. Slowly add the beer and stock, stirring constantly to prevent lumps forming in the cooking liquid. Add the thyme, bay leaf and browned beef, bring back up to the boil, then reduce the heat, cover with a lid and simmer gently for 2 hours or until the meat is tender.

3. After 90 minutes add the carrots and continue to cook for 30 minutes. Place in the pie dishes and leave to cool.

4. To make the pastry, mix the flour and salt with the suet and grated lard or butter in a large bowl. Mix in 150–175ml of water and knead for 1 minute or until you have a smooth dough.

5. On a lightly floured work surface, roll out the pastry to about 7mm (⅓in) thick and cut out 4 discs about 2cm (¾in) wider all the way round than the pie dishes. Brush the edges of the dishes with a little beaten egg and lay the pastry on top, crimping the edges using a fork or with your fingers and trimming away any excess pastry, then brush the top of the pies with the remaining beaten egg.

6. Bake in the oven for 40–50 minutes or until golden, then serve with buttered mashed potato and French beans.

SALMON AND MUSSEL PIE

I tend to use mash on this seafood pie, because puff pastry doesn't always cook properly. If you do prefer pastry though, you can substitute it, but don't cheat and do that rubbish dry dustbin lid plonked on the top, I hate that! A pie should have the filling and top cooked all together, as it tastes so much better when made as a whole. You can also leave out the capers and gherkins if you want.

SERVES 4

1–2 tbsp olive oil

500g (1lb 2oz) salmon fillet, pin bones and skin removed

1kg (2lb 3oz) mussels, cooked and removed from their shells

50g (2oz) gherkins, drained and chopped

25g (1oz) capers, drained

4 tsp chopped flat-leaf parsley

4 tsp chopped dill

4 tsp chopped chervil

3 banana shallots, peeled and finely sliced

200ml (7fl oz) double cream

Salt and black pepper

FOR THE MASH TOPPING

500g (1lb 2oz) large floury potatoes, such as King Edward, peeled and cut into quarters

50g (2oz) butter

100ml (3½fl oz) whole milk

ONE 20 X 30CM (8 X 12IN) PIE DISH OR OVENPROOF DISH

1. Preheat the oven to 170°C (325°F), Gas 3.

2. Cook and mash the potatoes for the topping following the instructions for Creamy Potato Mash on page 179.

3. While the potatoes are cooking, place a non-stick ovenproof pan over a medium heat, add the olive oil and the salmon and seal on both sides, then bake in the oven for about 8 minutes. Remove from the oven and allow to cool completely.

4. In a large bowl, mix together the mussel meat, gherkins, capers and herbs, then add the sliced shallots. Once the salmon is cool enough to handle, lift it from the pan and flake the meat into the bowl. (Some parts of the flesh may not be completely cooked but this doesn't matter as it will be fully cooked in the pie.) Mix all this together, then stir in the cream, season with salt and pepper and transfer to the pie dish.

5. Put the mashed potato into a piping bag and pipe it over the salmon mixture or spoon the potato over the top of the fish mix and spread it out evenly with a fork. Bake in the oven for 25 minutes or until the top of the pie is golden brown.

6. Remove the pie from the oven and serve with Minted Peas (see page 175).

SCALLOP AND FENNEL PIES

Why use pie dishes when the scallop shells look just as good? The best scallops for this are of course hand-dived: they are better for the environment, as dredging destroys the seabed and also fills the scallops with grit. Some of the best scallops I've eaten were from Scotland's west coast and from Ireland, but many are imported from America for some reason. Never freeze scallops, as they soak up water like a sponge and then when you cook them they dump all that water in the pan.

MAKES 4 'PIES'

4 large hand-dived scallops
1 fennel bulb
2 tbsp finely chopped chives
25g (1oz) butter
1 shallot, peeled and finely chopped
50ml (2fl oz) white wine
100ml (3½fl oz) double cream
100g (3½oz) ready-rolled all-butter puff pastry
1 egg, beaten
Salt and black pepper
Coarse sea salt, to serve

1. Preheat the oven to 200°C (400°F), Gas 6. Insert a sharp knife between the two halves of each scallop shell, then slice between the shells and pull them apart. Pull off the outer membrane and carefully remove the coral and white part of the scallop, dabbing them dry on kitchen paper.

2. Place the corals in a saucepan, add the top sprigs from the fennel bulb and half cover with water. Bring to the boil, then reduce the heat and simmer for 4–5 minutes. While the corals are cooking, clean and wash the scallop shells and, using a mandolin or a sharp knife, slice the fennel very thinly and set aside in a bowl with the chopped chives.

3. Melt the butter in a small frying pan and gently cook the shallot for 3–4 minutes or until softened but not browned. Add the white wine and drain the liquor from the cooked corals into the pan. Pour in the cream and bring to the boil. Boil until the liquid thickens, having reduced by about half, then season.

4. Place a pile of fennel and chives in each of the lower (more rounded) scallop shells, slice each scallop in half and place on top. Spoon over the sauce and cover with the top (flat) shells.

5. Lay out the pastry and cut into 4 strips each about 4 x 40cm (1½ x 16in). Using a little beaten egg, brush the edges of each pair of shells where they join and wrap a strip of pastry around the edges to seal the two halves together. Brush well with the remaining egg, then carefully place on a baking tray and bake in the oven for 10 minutes. Remove from the oven, place on a pile of sea salt and serve.

CHICKEN CURRY

I've worked with many Indian chefs over the years and it has been a privilege to learn from them, as Indian food can be so complex. Yuri, one of my head chefs, is great at quickly knocking up a simple curry. This is a dish we used to make towards the end of a night's service so that, after the guests had gone, the full team could sit down in the restaurant and dive in.

SERVES 4–6

1 tsp ground turmeric

1 tsp ground coriander

½ tsp ground cloves

50g (2oz) plain flour

1 large chicken, cut into 10 pieces (see method on pages 62–3)

3–4 tbsp vegetable oil

½ cinnamon stick

10 curry leaves

8 black peppercorns

1 onion, peeled and chopped

1 tbsp peeled and grated root ginger

1 x 400ml can of coconut milk

Salt and black pepper

1. Mix the ground spices and flour in a bowl and season with salt and pepper, then toss the chicken pieces in the spiced flour and set aside.

2. Place a large frying pan over a medium heat, add half the vegetable oil and fry the cinnamon stick, curry leaves and peppercorns for 30 seconds. Add the onion and ginger and fry for 5 minutes or until browned, then transfer to a bowl and put the pan back on the hob.

3. When the pan is hot again, pour in the remaining oil and seal the chicken pieces on all sides until browned. Add the onion and ginger back to the pan, stir in the coconut milk and simmer over a gentle heat for about 25–30 minutes or until the chicken is cooked through.

4. Remove from the heat, taste for seasoning and serve. This dish is great with broccoli and rice or even chips.

'Never hurry a good curry.'
VIVEK SINGH

CHAPTER 2
FISH

FILLETING A ROUND FISH

People often think there is a real art to this, and it can look much harder than it really is, especially when you watch a fishmonger do it. It's all about practice, so have a go and start with mackerel, as it's the easiest type to handle. Use a sharp knife – a filleting knife is best as it has a flexible blade. Whether the fish is small or large, it's the same method, so once you've done it a few times you'll start to get the hang of it.

1. First remove all the fins with a sharp pair of scissors, cutting as close as you can to the body of the fish. Holding it by the tail and using a palette knife or the back of a table knife, scrape the fish from the tail end towards the head to remove the scales. Tilt the knife slightly as you do this, being careful not to tear the skin.

2. Wash off the scales and pat dry with kitchen paper. Using a filleting knife (or other flexible knife), cut diagonally behind the gill to the bone.

3. Turn the knife around so that it is facing the tail, then cut through so that the flesh is on the top side of the knife while the bone is touching the underside. Keeping the knife close to the bone, cut horizontally towards the tail and through the belly bones, then lift off the fillet and set aside.

YOU WILL NEED

* *A round fish (such as mackerel)*
* *Kitchen scissors*
* *Palette knife or table knife*
* *Filleting knife*
* *Tweezers or small pliers*

4. Turn the fish over and repeat the process on the other side, then discard the carcass. (If you are filleting a non-oily fish, then the carcass can be reserved for making stock. The bones of oily fish are unsuitable for this purpose, however.)

5. Place the fillet skin side down with the fatter end facing you, then run your finger over the middle part. As you do so, you will feel the small pin bones, which can easily be removed using a pair of tweezers or small pair of pliers. Pull the bones towards you and discard.

6. Trim the edges of each fillet, removing any of the belly bones. Trying not to cut too much of the flesh away, cut the fillets into 150–175g (5–6oz) pieces and use as required.

FILLETING A FLAT FISH

This requires a little more practice than the previous technique and it's important you use the correct knife (with round fish you can get away with most sharp knives, but not for flat fish). A proper filleting knife is needed; it has a long flexible blade that enables you to cut through the fish keeping tight against the bones, leaving most of the flesh on the fillet and not too much remaining on the discarded skeleton. You can use a filleting knife for other jobs in the kitchen so a wise purchase won't go to waste. Remember that there are four fillets on a flat fish (as opposed to just two on a round fish).

1. Lay the fish on a chopping board with the head facing away from you, then trim the skirt or frill off the fish using kitchen scissors.

2. Using a filleting knife, cut around the head and discard it. Feel for the backbone down the middle of the fish and cut along it.

3. Starting at the head end of the fish and keeping the point of the knife close to the bone, carefully slice the fillet away from the bone, angling the knife towards the bone as you cut down to the tail, then lift off the fillet.

YOU WILL NEED

* A flat fish (such as sole)
* Kitchen scissors
* Filleting knife

4. Cut away the other fillet and then turn the fish over and repeat the process. Retain the carcass (but not the head) for making stock.

5. To remove the skin, lay a fillet skin side down with the tail end facing you. Holding the tip of the tail with your fingers and angling the knife down towards the skin, start to cut the flesh away from the skin.

6. Keeping a tight hold of the skin and using the knife in a sawing motion, continue to cut, keeping the knife at the same angle and cutting as close to the skin as possible until all the skin has been removed. Repeat with the remaining fillets.

SMOKED FISH PÂTÉ

Fish pâté is so easy to make – simply add cream and lemon to the picked meat and serve alongside warm toast for a great meal. I've made this one with Arbroath Smokies, but it can also be made from smoked mackerel.

SERVES 4

2 Arbroath Smokies or cooked kippers, skin and bones removed

Juice of 2 lemons

150ml (5fl oz) double cream

25g (1oz) chives, finely chopped

Sea salt and black pepper

FOUR 250ML (9FL OZ) RAMEKINS OR LITTLE POTS

1. Place the fish flesh in a blender and briefly pulse, then add the lemon juice and the double cream and purée to the desired consistency. (Don't leave the machine running for too long, however, or the cream may split.)

2. Transfer the pâté to a bowl, add the chives and season well. Divide between the ramekins or little pots and smooth over the surface. (If making these the day before, it is best to spread a little softened butter over the top of each one before refrigerating.)

3. Serve with warm slices of brown bread and a little dressed watercress on the side.

'At the end of a long day a good chef might think about giving it all up and doing something else. Next morning he'd be marvelling at a sleek, silver, line-caught bass or sniffing a big bunch of basil or thinking how he was going to sear those scallops and serve them with Iberico ham and lentils for lunch. It's not a perfect job, but what is?!'
RICK STEIN

BAKED ARBROATH SMOKIES WITH LEMON AND PARSLEY BUTTER

I first tried these little fellas at a Scottish coastal market. The Smokies are cleaned and marinated overnight in salted brine, then hot-smoked over a hardwood fire covered with wet sacks to stop the wood catching alight. They are a true delight served with butter. You need to get to the market early if you want one, as word gets around that they're cooking and people follow the smoke like zombies. To beat the queue, you can buy them online. Iain R Spinks is the best supplier I know, give him a bell and you won't be disappointed.

SERVES 4

4 Arbroath Smokies

2 lemons, cut into
wedges, to serve

**FOR THE LEMON
AND PARSLEY BUTTER**
250g (9oz) unsalted
butter, softened

Juice and grated zest
of 3 lemons

3 tbsp chopped
flat-leaf parsley

Sea salt and black pepper

1. Preheat the oven to 220°C (425°F), Gas 7, and cut out four 30cm (12in) squares of greaseproof paper and four of newspaper.

2. In a bowl, mix together all the ingredients for the lemon and parsley butter, seasoning the mixture with 2 teaspoons of salt and some pepper.

3. Place a greaseproof paper square on top of a square of newspaper. Put a fish in the centre of the greaseproof square, then spread a quarter of the lemon and parsley butter over the sides of the fish and fill the cavity.

4. Fold in the edges of the paper, roll into a parcel and tie up with string. Repeat the process with the other 3 fish and place them on a baking tray. (At this stage you could place them in the fridge for 6–8 hours or until you need them.)

5. Before cooking, sprinkle the parcels with a little water and then bake in the oven for 15 minutes. Remove from the oven and serve whole at the table with the lemon wedges and some slices of brown bread and butter.

SESAME TIGER PRAWNS WITH SPICED CUCUMBER AND CORIANDER SALAD

This is such a simple dish, which uses pre-cooked tiger prawns and can be served hot or cold. There has been a lot of bad press about tiger prawns over the years and the exploitation of farmers in countries like Vietnam where there are produced. The prawns will say on the packet where they are from, so my advice is to look for Madagascan prawns, as they have a better history in sustainable prawn farming. Ones from Ecuador are fine too, and this is the only country where they are certified organic.

SERVES 4

100g (3½oz) sesame seeds

3 tbsp English mustard

24 tiger prawns, peeled
and heads removed

1 red chilli, deseeded
and finely diced

50g (2oz) pickled ginger
with some of its juice

Grated zest and juice
of 2 limes

5 tbsp olive oil

1 cucumber, peeled

25g (1oz) unsalted butter

1 frisée lettuce

Leaves from 25g (1oz)
bunch of coriander

1. Spread the sesame seeds out on a plate and spoon the mustard into a bowl, then roll the tiger prawns first in the mustard and then in the sesame seeds, making sure that they are well coated, and set aside.

2. Place the chilli in a large bowl, then add the ginger and its juice, the lime zest and juice and 4 tablespoons of the olive oil and mix together well. Using a potato peeler, peel the cucumber into strips. (Don't peel all the way down to the seeds – the core can be discarded.) Add the cucumber strips to the chilli mixture, then toss all the ingredients together.

3. Place a non-stick frying pan over a medium heat, add the remaining olive oil and the prawns, frying these on each side for about 3 minutes or until golden brown. Add the butter and remove from the heat.

4. Break up the frisée lettuce and add the leaves to the cucumber salad along with the coriander, toss together and divide between plates. Place 6 prawns on each plate, then spoon over some of the chilli and lime dressing and serve.

CHILLI SALT SQUID

It was in Singapore that I first tried chilli-flavoured food done properly, with their trademark dish, the chilli crab. The traditional method is to roll the fish and cook in sticky chilli sauce, but for this squid recipe I prefer to deep-fry it with cornflour dusted over the top to make it lovely and crisp. Alternatively, you could chargrill it without the cornflour or fry it in a hot pan, but whichever method you use, the squid needs to be cooked as quickly as possible for best results.

SERVES 4

500g (1lb 2oz) squid, cleaned and tentacles removed

75g (3oz) cornflour

2–3 tbsp vegetable or sunflower oil

3 spring onions, thinly sliced

1 red bird's eye chilli, thinly sliced

Sea salt and black pepper

FOR THE DIPPING SAUCE

150ml (5fl oz) rice wine vinegar

100g (3½oz) caster sugar

2 red bird's eye chillies, thinly sliced

1 clove of garlic, peeled and finely chopped

1 tbsp chopped coriander

1 shallot, peeled and finely chopped

1. To make the sauce, place the vinegar, sugar, chillies and garlic in a heavy-based saucepan and bring to the boil, then reduce the heat and simmer until the sauce thickens and a syrup is formed. Remove from the heat, add the coriander and shallot and set aside.

2. To prepare the squid, split each tube down the middle and lightly score the surface in a criss-cross pattern, then cut into 2.5cm (1in) pieces and dust with the cornflour.

3. Place a large, non-stick wok or frying pan over a medium heat, add a little of the vegetable or sunflower oil and, frying the squid pieces in batches and using more oil as necessary, cook for about 2 minutes or until golden brown, then remove from the wok or pan and season with salt and pepper.

4. Place the squid in a serving bowl, sprinkle over the spring onions, chilli and more black pepper and serve with the dipping sauce.

CRAB WITH RAPESEED MAYONNAISE AND WATERCRESS

Often (wrongly) described as the poor man's lobster, I personally think the flavour of crab is far better than its expensive cousin. While crab has been eaten for thousands of years, rapeseed oil is much newer. Traditionally, rapeseed was animal food, or turned into Biofuel, but some clever dick decided to press the oil from this bright yellow flower and the result is brilliant for dressings and for cooking with. It's also much cheaper than olive oil. Rapeseed oil gives mayonnaise a nicer flavour and colour than usual.

SERVES 4

100g (3½oz) watercress

3 tbsp rapeseed oil

900g (2lb) white (or mixed white and dark) cooked crab meat (preferably Portland) or 1.3kg (3lb) cooked crab claws

Salt and black pepper

2 lemons, cut into wedges, to serve

FOR THE MAYONNAISE
3 egg yolks
2 tsp Dijon mustard
375ml (13fl oz) rapeseed oil
Juice of 1 lemon

1. First make the mayonnaise. Whisk together the egg yolks and mustard very thoroughly in a blender or in a bowl using an electric beater or hand whisk. Add the rapeseed oil drop by drop to start with and then in a steady flow, and keep blending or whisking until the mayonnaise has thickened. Add the lemon juice and season to taste with salt and pepper.

2. Place the watercress in a bowl, add the rapeseed oil and season with salt and pepper. Toss together and place some on each plate along with a pile of the crab meat or a pile of crab claws. Spoon some mayonnaise on the side and serve with a couple of lemon wedges.

GRILLED BUTTERFLIED SARDINES WITH BLACK OLIVE AND HERB DRESSING

Sardines must be the world's most commonly eaten fish and every country seems to have a famous version. I first tried them in France, aged 14. Brittany is thought to be the place where canning sardines began, and there are still masses of canneries in the area. As with most oily fish, they're best eaten as fresh as possible. The eyes should be bright and shiny, the gills a nice red colour and the skin not dry. Removing the bones and head is easy for your fishmonger to do and will save you a load of mess and fiddling about at home.

SERVES 4

7 tbsp olive oil

12 sardines, scales removed (ask your fishmonger to remove the backbone and head)

2 cloves of garlic, peeled and crushed

2 shallots, peeled and finely diced

2 sprigs of thyme, chopped

100g (3½oz) mixed salad leaves

Salt and black pepper

FOR THE DRESSING

30ml (1¼fl oz) red wine vinegar

1 tsp caster sugar

50g (2oz) pitted black olives, cut into quarters

150ml (5fl oz) rapeseed oil

4 tsp chopped flat-leaf parsley

2 tsp chopped chives

1. Drizzle 1 tablespoon of the olive oil into a non-stick roasting tin and place the sardines on it, skin side up, then season with salt and pepper.

2. In a bowl, mix together the garlic, shallots and thyme with the remaining oil, then spoon over the top of the sardines and leave to marinate for 15 minutes.

3. Preheat the grill to medium or the oven to 170°C (325°F), Gas 3.

4. Place the sardines under the grill or in the oven and cook for 4–5 minutes, without turning.

5. While the sardines are cooking, make the dressing. Pour the vinegar into a bowl and add the sugar, allowing it to dissolve. Add the olives, rapeseed oil and herbs, mix together and set aside.

6. Arrange the salad leaves on individual plates, then remove the sardines from the grill or oven and place 3 on top of each portion of salad. Drizzle over the dressing and serve with crusty bread.

SALT-CRUSTED SEA BASS

You may look daft buying this much salt; people may think you're stocking up for an icy garden path. Little do they know it's actually for this dish, one of the best ways to bring out all the flavour of sea bass. If you can't find good bass (they are farmed now, so generally not too pricey) you can use trout. It must be sea salt, not fine table salt – use that for the path and keep the good stuff for your food. Cracking the crust at the table is quite an event. The fish doesn't end up tasting salty, it's just pure, white, delicious flesh.

SERVES 2

1.2kg (2lb 10oz) sea salt

3 egg whites

1 small bunch of dill, stalks removed and reserved, leaves chopped

1 x 750g (1lb 10oz) whole sea bass, gutted, scales removed and head and tail cut off

Handful of edible seaweed

1. Preheat the oven to 200°C (400°F), Gas 6.

2. Place the sea salt in a large bowl and add the egg whites and chopped dill. Stuff the cavity of the fish with the reserved dill stalks.

3. Cover the bottom of a deep roasting tin with about one-third of the sea salt mixture and then scatter over the seaweed. Put the sea bass on top and cover with the remaining salt mixture, making sure the whole of the fish is covered, underneath as well as on top. Pat the fish down and then place in the oven to bake for 25 minutes or until the salt crust sounds hard when tapped with the back of a teaspoon.

4. Remove the tin from the oven and crack the salt crust to reveal the cooked fish – the skin should peel away easily. Serve with a salad of crisp lettuce leaves, such as Little Gem, tossed in olive oil and lemon juice.

'James has a knack for making food and recipes that are positively inspirational.'

KEN HOM

PROPER FISH AND CHIPS

If I were ever on Mastermind then I would choose this dish as my specialist subject! Over the years, I've sampled good and bad. I've travelled miles to get my hands on that crisp batter and pure white flesh, and once drove my team on a 500-mile round trip to prove that the best fish and chips were from my home county of Yorkshire. So this batter recipe is one that has been brought to you after eating many hundreds of fish and pounding thousands of miles, look after it and enjoy!

SERVES 4

1.2 litres (2 pints) vegetable oil, for deep-frying

4 large peeled potatoes (about 1.5kg/3lb 4oz)

4 x 175g (6oz) fillets of cod, haddock or pollack, pin bones removed

Salt

FOR THE BATTER

225g (8oz) self-raising flour

1 tsp salt

15g (½oz) fresh yeast or 20g (¾oz) dried yeast

2 tsp cider or white wine vinegar

1 tsp caster sugar

200ml (7fl oz) beer

1. To make the batter, sift the flour and salt into a bowl and add the yeast, vinegar and sugar, then whisk in the beer and, once combined, set aside for 45 minutes to 1 hour to bubble up.

2. If using a deep-fat fryer, heat the vegetable oil to 95°C (200°F). Alternatively, fill a deep, heavy-based saucepan to one-third with oil and use a sugar thermometer to check that it has reached the correct temperature. (Take great care if using a saucepan: always watch over it and never fill it beyond more than a third as the hot fat may bubble up when the food is added.)

3. Trim the potatoes into rectangles, cut into slices 1cm (½in) thick, then cut again to give chips that are 1cm (½in) wide. Place the chips in the deep-fat fryer or saucepan and cook for 10 minutes. (It is very important to pre-cook them in this way to ensure that they are cooked through before serving. Frying the chips at this temperature will blanch them without browning.)

4. Check the chips are tender using the point of a knife, then remove from the oil and drain on kitchen paper. They can be left to cool on greaseproof paper and even chilled before finishing.

5. Preheat the oil in the fryer or pan to 190°C (375°F). Immerse the fish fillets in the batter, then carefully lower into the hot oil and cook for 3–4 minutes or until golden brown. Remove from the oil and drain on kitchen paper, then reheat the oil to cook the chips.

6. Lower the chips into the oil. These will now take only 2–3 minutes to become golden brown and crispy. Shake off any excess fat, or drain on kitchen paper, and sprinkle with salt before serving with the fish.

SKATE WINGS WITH BLACK CAPER BUTTER

This is one of the classic butter sauces; the trick is the get the pan nice and hot before adding the butter. Once the butter is brown, pull the pan off the heat, add the rest of the ingredients and serve straight away. This sauce can be served with all manner of fish and seafood, from salmon and trout to hake and prawns. I've chosen to put it with skate wings, which are attractive and a bit different to serve up to your guests.

SERVES 2

2 x 225g (8oz) skate wings, skinned

FOR THE COOKING LIQUOR
1 onion, peeled and chopped into 2cm (¾in) pieces

2 sticks of celery, trimmed and chopped into 2cm (¾in) pieces

250ml (9fl oz) white wine

75ml (3fl oz) white wine vinegar

2 bay leaves

10 black peppercorns

Pinch of salt

FOR THE BLACK CAPER BUTTER
100g (3½oz) butter

25g (1oz) capers, drained and rinsed

50ml (2fl oz) red wine vinegar

2 tbsp chopped flat-leaf parsley

1. Place all the ingredients for the cooking liquor in a large saucepan, pour in 1.2 litres (2 pints) of water, bring to the boil, then reduce the heat and simmer gently for 10 minutes.

2. Place the skate wings in the pan and continue to simmer slowly for about 10 minutes to cook the fish. Using a slotted spoon, carefully lift the skate from the pan, then drain on kitchen paper and place on a plate in a warm oven while you make the black caper butter.

3. Melt the butter in a large frying pan over a high heat, allowing it to foam and turn brown. Remove from the heat and add the remaining ingredients. Let the mixture fizz in the pan for a few seconds and then spoon over the skate and serve straight away.

SAFFRON HADDOCK WITH CRUSHED POTATOES AND ASPARAGUS

Produced from the stigma of the crocus flower, saffron is the most expensive spice in the world. It takes some 70,000 flowers to make just half a kilo in weight of finished saffron. It's used in Biryani, Pilaf and many desserts, but is perhaps best known for its use in the French bouillabaisse and Spanish paella. In the UK, it's used in Cornish saffron cake. This recipe makes a light fish supper and the addition of saffron to the poaching liquid gives it a nice flavour, but be careful because too much will overpower everything else.

SERVES 4

500ml (18fl oz) milk

2 good pinches of saffron

4 x 150g (5oz) natural smoked haddock fillets, pin bones and skin removed

400g (14oz) new potatoes, unpeeled

50ml (2fl oz) double cream

2 tbsp chopped chives

4 tsp chopped dill

20 asparagus spears, woody ends snapped off

25g (1oz) unsalted butter

Salt and black pepper

1. Pour the milk into a roasting tin, add the saffron and place over a low heat to gently warm through and allow the flavour of the spice to infuse the milk. Add the haddock fillets and cook over a gentle heat for 3–4 minutes, then remove from the heat and leave the fish to sit in the milk until required.

2. Place the potatoes in a large saucepan of salted water and cook for 20 minutes or until tender, then drain. While the potatoes are still warm, add the double cream and, with a fork, crush the potatoes but without mashing them, then mix in the chopped herbs, season with salt and pepper and set aside.

3. Bring another saucepan of salted water to the boil, plunge the asparagus in and cook for 2 minutes or until tender, then drain, add the butter and arrange 5 spears on each plate. Gently warm the haddock in the milk, place a spoonful of potatoes next to the asparagus, then lift the haddock from the milk, place a fillet on top of each portion of potatoes and serve.

FISHCAKES WITH BUTTER SAUCE

A classic butter sauce is one of those recipes that, once you've mastered, you will use again and again. Yes, there's a shed-load of butter, but it's the richness that makes it go so well with all types of seafood. I remember I once spent two weeks just making this sauce over and over in the restaurant I was working in at the time. It was worth all that practice, as I use the same method even now. The sauce can be flavoured with all manner of ingredients from tomato to orange, just change the flavour to suit yourself.

SERVES 4–6

300ml (11fl oz) milk

1 x 200g (7oz) natural smoked haddock fillet

1 x 225g (8oz) salmon fillet

115g (4oz) butter

350g (12oz) mashed potatoes (following method on page 179 but using no butter or cream)

2 small onions, peeled and diced

3 tbsp chopped flat-leaf parsley

2 tbsp chopped dill

150g (5oz) plain flour

2 eggs, beaten

150g (5oz) dried breadcrumbs, such as Japanese panko

2 tbsp vegetable oil

Salt and black pepper

FOR THE BUTTER SAUCE

150ml (5fl oz) white wine

250ml (9fl oz) fish stock

1 shallot, peeled and sliced

150ml (5fl oz) double cream

50g (2oz) butter, chilled and diced

2 tsp chopped dill

1. Pour the milk into a large saucepan, season with salt and pepper and place over a low heat to warm through. Poach the haddock and salmon in the milk for 3–4 minutes or until cooked through. Remove from the milk and allow to cool.

2. Meanwhile, melt 75g (3oz) of the butter in a small saucepan.

3. When the haddock and salmon are cool enough to handle, flake the flesh of each fish separately, discarding the skin and any bones. Place the haddock in a large bowl, add the potatoes, onions and melted butter and mix together. Add the salmon and chopped herbs and mix again until combined, but without over-mixing. Season with salt and pepper to taste, adding a little of the haddock poaching milk if the mixture seems too dry.

4. Divide the mixture into 4 equal portions, then shape into patties. Dip in the flour, the beaten eggs and finally the breadcrumbs and then chill in the fridge for 2 hours before frying.

5. Place a frying pan over a medium heat, add the vegetable oil and the remaining butter and fry the fishcakes on each side for 3–4 minutes or until golden brown.

6. While the fishcakes are cooking, make the sauce. Place the wine, stock and shallot in a saucepan and boil for about 5 minutes to reduce by half. Pour in the cream, bring back up to the boil, then remove from the heat and whisk in the diced butter. Stir in the dill, season with salt and pepper and serve with the fishcakes, spooning a little on to each plate along with a handful of watercress leaves or some wilted spinach.

MISO-BLACKENED BREAM WITH CARAMELISED CHICORY

Miso is a Japanese paste made from soya beans fermented with rice or barley. You will find several varieties of miso in the shops – some are light in colour and some are dark. The darker the colour, the stronger the flavour tends to be so I use the lighter colours for a milder result. Combined with the rest of the ingredients, and used to marinate the fish, the miso will cause the fish to brown more under the grill. It should be cooked quickly and the blackened bits left on it, as they add to the flavour of the finished dish.

SERVES 4

3–4 tbsp groundnut oil, plus extra for drizzling

4 x 125g (4½oz) black bream fillets (preferably Dorset bream), scales and pin bones removed

325g (11½oz) white miso paste

50ml (2fl oz) rice vinegar

50ml (2fl oz) mirin

50g (2oz) caster sugar

75g (3oz) mizuna leaves, to serve

FOR THE CARAMELISED CHICORY

2 chicory bulbs, cut into quarters lengthways through the root

200g (7oz) caster sugar

2 tbsp olive oil

1. Preheat the grill to high.

2. Rub the groundnut oil into the bream fillets and set aside. Place the miso paste, rice vinegar, mirin and caster sugar in a large bowl and mix well, then immerse the bream in this mixture. Remove the fillets from the bowl, lay them on a baking tray and leave to marinate for 20 minutes.

3. Meanwhile, place the chicory and sugar in a separate bowl and toss together. Set a non-stick frying pan over a medium heat, add the olive oil and the sugared chicory and allow to caramelise for 10–15 minutes or until golden brown all over. Remove from the pan and allow to cool slightly, then place on individual plates.

4. Place the bream under the grill and cook for 4–5 minutes. The marinade will start to blacken, but don't be tempted to turn the fish over. To check whether the fish is done, gently press your finger into one fillet: if it penetrates, the fish is cooked; if not, return the bream to the grill for another couple of minutes.

5. Slide the bream from the tray and place on top of the chicory. Top with a few of the mizuna leaves, drizzle over a little of the groundnut oil and serve.

TROUT WITH FENNEL, BLOOD ORANGE AND ALMOND AÏOLI

I always think trout is a fish that gets overlooked in shops and supermarkets. I love the stuff, either the big brown wild trout, or the farmed rainbow variety. This fish will take grilling, poaching or frying, and will stand up to quite strong flavours too, such as the fennel in this salad. Almonds are a classic accompaniment to trout and can either be toasted and added to the sauce, or sprinkled over the salad.

SERVES 4

1 fennel bulb, thinly sliced

Peeled segments and leftover juice of 2 blood oranges

4–5 tbsp extra-virgin olive oil

2 trout, filleted and skin removed

25g (1oz) unsalted butter

4 tsp chopped dill

Salt and black pepper

100g (3½oz) micro salad leaves, to serve

FOR THE AÏOLI

15g (½oz) butter

50g (2oz) flaked almonds

2 cloves of garlic, peeled and crushed

2 tbsp white wine vinegar

4 tsp Dijon mustard

2 egg yolks

150ml (5fl oz) rapeseed oil

1. Place the sliced fennel in a bowl, add the orange segments and pour over the juice, season with salt and pepper, drizzle over half the olive oil and set aside.

2. Next make the aïoli. Melt the butter in a small pan set over a high heat, add the almonds and sauté for 2–3 minutes or until lightly browned. As soon as they turn brown, remove the nuts from the pan to prevent them burning.

3. Place the garlic and vinegar in the pan and gently warm through, then remove from the heat and place in a blender with the mustard and toasted almonds. Whizz to a purée then add the egg yolks and mix until well combined. With the machine still running, slowly add the rapeseed oil, a little at a time, until it is all incorporated. (If the mixture seems too thick, add a little water.) Transfer the aïoli to a bowl and set aside.

4. Place a non-stick frying pan over a medium heat, add the remaining olive oil and the trout fillets and cook on one side for 3–4 minutes or until golden brown, then turn over and add the butter, allowing it to melt. Season with salt and pepper, remove from the heat and leave to rest for 1–2 minutes.

5. Add the chopped dill to the fennel and orange mixture and toss together, then arrange a few segments on each plate and place some fennel slices on top. Lay a trout fillet on the fennel, scatter with salad leaves, drizzle over some of the orange juice and olive oil and serve with the almond aïoli.

TERIYAKI MACKEREL FILLETS WITH WILTED SPINACH

In the west we tend to put teriyaki with chicken, but in Japan it is normally used for fish like tuna, salmon or trout. I once had teriyaki smoked eel and foie gras in a Japanese restaurant. However, foie gras isn't always considered ethical, and eel is as rare as rocking horse pooh to get hold of where I live, so I use mackerel instead. The word teriyaki means 'shine', or 'lustre', and 'boiling' and ultimately that's what should happen. The meat should have a deep clear glaze and be completely coated in the sauce.

SERVES 4

2 tbsp olive oil

8 mackerel fillets, skin on and pin bones removed

100g (3½oz) wilted spinach (see method on page 96)

Salt and black pepper

FOR THE TERIYAKI SAUCE

50ml (2fl oz) dark soy sauce

50ml (2fl oz) mirin

25ml (1fl oz) sake

15g (½oz) caster sugar

1. Combine together in a bowl all the ingredients for the teriyaki sauce and set aside.

2. Place a non-stick frying pan over a medium heat, add the olive oil then season the mackerel with salt and pepper and add to the pan. Fry the fillets on one side for about 3–4 minutes or until the edges start to turn golden brown, then turn over and remove from the heat.

3. Pour over the teriyaki sauce, spooning it over the fillets until the pan decreases in temperature. Place the wilted spinach in the centre of each plate, lay 2 mackerel fillets on top, drizzle over a little of the sauce and serve.

STEAMED MUSSELS WITH CIDER, SPRING ONIONS AND CREAM

It's amazing to see mussels being grown. They grow on ropes some 15–20 metres long and, as they get bigger, the ropes are lifted out of the water sometimes daily and pruned to prevent new small mussels from forming. Getting rid of these small ones allows the rest to grow bigger. Once you've cooked this dish, any unopened mussels should always be discarded as they are not good to eat.

SERVES 2

900g (2lb) live mussels (preferably Shetland)

50g (2oz) butter

8 spring onions, chopped into 2cm (¾in) pieces

2 cloves of garlic, peeled and finely diced

250ml (9fl oz) cider (preferably scrumpy) or perry

4 sprigs of thyme

300ml (11fl oz) double cream

25g (1oz) flat-leaf parsley, roughly chopped

Salt and black pepper

1. Wash the mussels in a colander to remove any dirt or grit. Pick through them, removing any stringy 'beard' from the shells. If any of the mussels are slightly open, tap them on the work surface to see if they close (which means they're still alive) and discard any that remain open.

2. Melt the butter in a large heavy-based saucepan and sauté the spring onions and garlic over a high heat for 1 minute before pouring in the cider or perry. Add the thyme and the mussels, place a lid on the pan and cook for 3–4 minutes or until the mussels start to open.

3. Add the cream, season with salt and pepper and add the parsley, stirring it in with a wooden spoon.

4. Divide the mussels between bowls, discarding any that haven't opened during cooking. Pour over the sauce and any spring onions left in the pan and serve.

SALMON WITH SALSA VERDE

The best way to make this classic sauce is to chop all the ingredients by hand to really combine the flavours. This is the Italian version and shouldn't be confused with the French Sauce Verte, which is mayonnaise-based and flavoured with tarragon and parsley. Salsa Verde can be made in advance and kept for up to 4 days in the fridge.

SERVES 4

Olive oil, for cooking

4 x 150g (5oz) salmon fillets, skin on and pin bones removed

25g (1oz) butter

FOR THE SALSA VERDE

3 spring onions, chopped

Grated zest and juice of 1½ lemons

25g (1oz) gherkins, drained and rinsed

25g (1oz) capers, drained and rinsed

2 tsp chopped flat-leaf parsley

2 tsp chopped chervil

2 tsp chopped mint

1 tsp chopped thyme leaves

150ml (5fl oz) extra-virgin olive oil

Salt and black pepper

1. Place a non-stick frying pan over a medium heat, add the olive oil and the salmon fillets and cook for 2–3 minutes on one side. Add the butter and turn the salmon over, spooning the melted butter over the fish, and continue to cook for another 2–3 minutes, then remove from the heat and allow to rest in the pan.

2. To make the salsa verde, place the spring onions in a blender along with the lemon juice and zest, gherkins, capers and herbs. Purée together and, while the machine is running, slowly add the olive oil to form a paste. Transfer to a bowl and season with salt and pepper.

3. Remove the salmon from the pan and place a fillet on each plate, then spoon over some of the salsa verde and serve with a crisp salad or wilted spinach (see page 54).

TANDOORI COD STEAKS

It's a bit cheeky calling it this really, as the word tandoor actually refers to the cylindrical-shaped oven in which Indian food is cooked – in particular naan breads. But tandoori cooking and its flavours are famous all over the world, and though they're normally associated with chicken, I love them with fish. Firm, meaty fish like cod, salmon and monkfish lend themselves best to the flavours.

SERVES 4

4 x 200g (7oz) cod steaks
Vegetable oil, for oiling
Sprigs of coriander, to garnish
2 limes, cut in half, to serve

FOR THE TANDOORI SPICE MIX
2 tsp whole cumin seeds
2 tsp coriander seeds
3 tsp fennel seeds
1 tsp cayenne pepper
1 tsp ground turmeric
Juice of 1 lemon
75g (3oz) plain yoghurt
4 tsp peeled and
grated root ginger
1 shallot, peeled and chopped
2 tbsp chopped coriander
2 cloves of garlic, peeled
½ tsp salt

1. To make the tandoori spice mixture, first grind the whole seeds in a spice grinder or coffee grinder or using a pestle and mortar. Place all the remaining ingredients in a blender, add the freshly ground spices and blend for 1 minute.

2. Place the cod steaks in a bowl and coat in the spice mixture, cover with cling film and leave in the fridge for 1–2 hours to marinate.

3. Preheat the grill to medium and lightly oil a baking tray that will fit under the grill.

4. Lay the cod on the tray, pouring over any marinade left in the bowl. Place under the grill for 10 minutes (the fillets should cook through without needing to turn them over), then remove from the grill, garnish with coriander sprigs and serve with the fresh lime halves and some boiled basmati rice.

WHISKY-MARINATED SALMON WITH BEETROOT

Many of my ideas come from watching and working with other chefs; as the old saying goes, you never stop learning, no matter how old you are. This recipe was inspired by a mate of mine, John Campbell, a 2-Michelin-star boy with some really brilliant ideas, of which this is one. I've taken the idea and made it a little simpler for you. It might seem like there are some odd flavours here, but eaten as a whole they work really well together.

SERVES 4

4 salmon supremes, pin bones and skin removed

50g (2oz) salt

60g (2½oz) caster sugar

200ml (7fl oz) whisky

100ml (3½fl oz) rice vinegar

100ml (3½fl oz) white wine vinegar

2 banana shallots, peeled and finely sliced

400ml (14fl oz) sunflower oil or duck fat

TO SERVE

4 cooked beetroot (not in vinegar), peeled and sliced

75g (3oz) mixed salad leaves

2 tbsp coriander leaves

1. Place the salmon on a baking tray, cover with the salt and 50g (2oz) of the sugar, drizzle over the whisky and set aside for 2 hours to marinate. Then wash off the marinade, pat dry with kitchen paper or a clean tea towel and set aside.

2. Pour the rice and white wine vinegars into a saucepan, add the remaining sugar and gently warm through, then tip in the sliced shallots, remove from the heat and allow to cool.

3. Add the sunflower oil or duck fat to a heavy-based frying pan and heat to 65°C (149°F), measuring the temperature using a sugar thermometer, then remove from the heat. Place the marinated salmon fillets in the pan, cover with a lid and leave for 7 minutes, then remove the salmon from the pan, drain and pat dry.

4. Arrange slices of the beetroot on each plate, then place a small pile of salad leaves on top, along with some of the marinated shallots. Lay a salmon fillet on top, scatter over a few coriander leaves, drizzle over some of the vinegar marinade and serve.

CHAPTER 3
POULTRY

10 PIECE CHICKEN CUT

Cutting a chicken into pieces is so simple and requires only basic knife skills as there are hardly any bones to cut though. The advantage of doing this with a whole chicken is that you are left with the carcass, which can be used to make great stock.

1. Place the chicken breast-side up with the neck towards you, cut off any excess skin from the neck and, using a small sharp knife, remove the wish bone just under the skin. Then cut off both wings at the joint that attaches them to the breasts.

2. Turn the chicken over and look for the joint that connects the thigh to the chicken. Using the sharp knife, cut through the joint, rather than the bone itself, and repeat for the other leg.

3. Then cut these pieces in two through the joint linking the drumstick and thigh, giving you two thighs and two leg pieces.

YOU WILL NEED
* * A whole chicken
* * Poultry shears or kitchen scissors
* * Small sharp knife

4. Using poultry shears or a pair of sharp scissors, remove the backbone and ribcage. This is done by cutting down both sides of the breast so that the ribs and backbone come away in one piece. Carefully cut with one hand and pull with the other to ensure that as little meat as possible still adheres to the carcass.

5. Discard the backbone or retain for making stock (see pages 64–5). Slice down through the breastbone to separate the breasts.

6. Finally, cut both breasts in half crossways. You now have 10 pieces of chicken.

BROWN CHICKEN STOCK

Stock is the basis of all good cooking, and is made day in, day out, come rain or shine, in every good commercial kitchen all over the world. Most meat sauces are made with stock and the way your sauce turns out depends on the way you make the stock in the first place. For chicken stock, if you brown the bones in the oven first, you will end up with brown chicken stock; if you don't, and place them straight in the pan with water, you will have standard (white) chicken stock. (So to make 'standard' chicken stock – useful in so many dishes – follow the recipe below but omit the tomato purée and ignore steps 1–2 for roasting the bones and vegetables.) Whichever type you make, you should always reduce the stock before use to thicken the texture and increase the flavour. Both varieties can be kept in the fridge in an airtight container for 3–4 days or frozen for later use.

1. Preheat the oven to 230°C (450°F), Gas 8. Place all the chicken bones on a large baking tray and mix in the tomato purée and the vegetables.

2. Bake in the oven for 30–40 minutes or until nicely browned.

3. Remove from the oven and tip the bones and vegetables into a large, heavy-based saucepan. Add the peppercorns and thyme, pour in 2.5 litres (4⅓ pints) of water and bring to a rapid boil.

MAKES ABOUT 1.5 LITRES (2½ PINTS)

* *2kg (4lb 6oz) chicken bones*
* *3 tbsp tomato purée*
* *1 large white onion, peeled and roughly chopped*
* *2 carrots, peeled and roughly chopped*
* *½ leek, trimmed and roughly chopped*
* *6 black peppercorns*
* *2 sprigs of thyme*
* *10 ice cubes*

4. When the water has come to the boil, reduce the heat and simmer for about 1½ hours. To achieve a clear stock, you'll need to keep skimming off any foam that forms on top. Adding the ice cubes will help to solidify the fat, making it easier to remove.

5. Remove from the heat and allow to cool. Once cool strain the stock though a fine sieve and leave in the fridge until cold.

6. Skim off any remaining fat and you have a fresh brown chicken stock that's ready to use.

CLUB SANDWICH WITH SMOKED BACON MAYONNAISE

The traditional club sandwich was always made with turkey, but now it can be found containing beef, chicken and even ham. It's thought to have been invented by a chef in a New York casino in the late 19th century, which is probably true, given the usual portion size. I love making smoked bacon mayonnaise to put with this – yes, it sounds a bit fancy, but so did smoky bacon flavoured crisps when they first came out and look at them now. It's essentially just mayonnaise with bacon bits in it, but the flavour is great.

SERVES 4

4 x 200g (7oz) skinless and boneless cooked chicken breasts (preferably corn-fed)

4 baguettes

50g (2oz) butter

2 Little Gem lettuces

4 spring onions

FOR THE SMOKED BACON MAYONNAISE

2 egg yolks

½ tbsp English mustard

1 tbsp white wine vinegar

200ml (7fl oz) rapeseed oil, plus extra for frying

8 smoked bacon rashers

4 tbsp chopped chives

Salt and black pepper

1. To make the mayonnaise, place the egg yolks in a bowl with the mustard and vinegar. Using an electric beater or hand whisk, whisk the yolks for 2 minutes before slowly adding the rapeseed oil, drop by drop to start with and then in a steady flow. Keep whisking until all the oil has been used up and the mayonnaise is thick and creamy, then season with salt and pepper.

2. Place the bacon rashers in a sieve, pour over half a kettle of boiling water and place on kitchen paper to dry. Then cut the bacon into 2.5cm (1in) pieces.

3. Place a small frying pan over a high heat, add a little rapeseed oil and fry the bacon pieces for 2–3 minutes or until golden brown. Remove from the pan, drain on more kitchen paper and allow to cool.

4. Slice the chicken breast thinly, then cut the baguettes in half and butter them. Break off the lettuce leaves and place on 4 of the buttered baguette halves. Slice the spring onions and place on top, followed by the slices of cooked chicken.

5. Combine the bacon and chives with the mayonnaise and spoon over the chicken. Top with the remaining baguette halves, then cut each sandwich in half and serve.

QUICK CHICKEN WITH GARLIC BEANS AND CHORIZO

This is the kind of food that chefs love – quick to prepare but with masses of flavour. Take away the chicken and essentially you have posh beans on toast. The type of chorizo you need for this dish is the one that comes in sausage-form and needs to be cooked (chorizo picante), rather than the thinly sliced, ready-to-eat type. It has extra paprika to give it more spice and flavour. I like to source my garlic from the brilliant Garlic Farm on the Isle of Wight, if you want to give it a try their products can be bought online.

SERVES 4

25ml (1fl oz) extra-virgin olive oil

4 x 175g (6oz) boneless chicken breasts (preferably corn-fed), with the skin on

1 bulb of garlic, cut in half crossways

250g (9oz) raw chorizo sausage, diced

2 shallots, peeled and finely chopped

2 sprigs of rosemary

1 x 300g can of haricot beans, drained and rinsed

150ml (5fl oz) chicken stock (see pages 64–5)

25g (1oz) butter

25g (1oz) flat-leaf parsley, chopped

Salt and black pepper

1. Preheat the oven to 200°C (400°F), Gas 6.

2. Place a large frying pan over a high heat and pour in half the olive oil. Season the chicken breasts well with salt and pepper, add to the pan and fry on each side for 2–3 minutes or until golden brown. Place on a baking tray, add the halves of garlic bulb and drizzle with the pan juices, then bake in the oven for 12 minutes or until cooked through.

3. While the chicken is cooking, place the pan back over the heat, add the remaining oil and the chorizo and fry for 2–3 minutes. Add the shallots, rosemary, beans and stock and bring to the boil, then reduce the heat and simmer, uncovered, for 10 minutes.

4. Remove the chicken from the oven and allow to rest, then remove the garlic and squeeze out the flesh from the inside. Chop the flesh well with a knife and add to the beans. Stir in the butter and parsley and season well with salt and pepper.

5. Spoon the beans on to individual plates with the chicken sliced on the top, drizzle with the pan juices and serve.

ROASTED CHICKEN WITH SUGARED CARROTS AND TURNIPS

Who doesn't like a roast chicken (apart from vegetarians, that is!)? There is something irresistible about a plain roast chicken and this recipe takes it even further with simple vegetables like turnips and carrots that work so well alongside the bird. Free-range organic chickens and the corn-fed type are of course the best for flavour, but look out for chickens with an RSPCA badge on the packet, as these are great too and a little cheaper.

SERVES 4

30ml (1¼fl oz) olive oil

4 x 200g (7oz) boneless chicken breasts (preferably corn-fed), with the skin on

8 streaky bacon rashers

250g (9oz) Chantenay carrots

250g (9oz) baby turnips, trimmed

25g (1oz) caster sugar

75g (3oz) butter

25g (1oz) chopped chervil or chives

Salt and black pepper

1. Preheat the oven to 200°C (400°F), Gas 6.

2. Place a large, ovenproof frying pan over a high heat and add the olive oil. Season the chicken breasts well with salt and pepper, then add to the pan and fry on each side for 2–3 minutes to give a nice golden-brown colour.

3. Top each of the chicken breasts with 2 bacon rashers twisted together and roast in the oven for 12–14 minutes or until cooked through.

4. Place the carrots and turnips in a large, wide saucepan. Add the sugar and butter and 1 teaspoon of salt, then fill the pan with water so that it comes three-quarters of the way up the vegetables. Bring to the boil and, keeping on a high heat, rapidly boil for 10 minutes or until the liquid reduces to the point where a sauce is made out of the pan juices. The idea behind this is that as the liquid reduces it cooks the vegetables, leaving a sweet buttery emulsion in the pan.

5. Remove the chicken from the oven and allow to rest, then remove the bacon rashers (setting these aside) and slice each breast into 4 pieces.

6. To finish the carrots and turnips, add the chopped chervil or chives, season with salt and pepper and spoon into individual dishes with a sliced chicken breast on top. Add the crispy bacon, drizzle over the juices from the vegetable pan and serve.

CHICKEN IN A PARMESAN, ALMOND AND THYME CRUMB

This was a hit the very first time I tried it in my test kitchen. The idea came from veal cooked in a similar way. The nuts and cheese prevent the breadcrumb coating from being too dry and the secret is to cook it in plenty of butter. Yes, we all know how I love my butter, but this dish will prove my point, as it helps the chicken to cook more evenly and to colour nicely. If you want, you can use hazelnuts instead of almonds for the crumb. Serve with plenty of lemon chunks and dive in.

SERVES 4

4 x 200g (7oz) skinless and boneless chicken breasts

2 eggs

100g (3½oz) plain flour

100g (3½oz) butter

Salt and black pepper

FOR THE CRUMB

100g (3½oz) almonds, toasted (see method on page 53)

100g (3½oz) dried breadcrumbs, such as Japanese panko

75g (3oz) Parmesan cheese, finely grated

Grated zest of 4 lemons

Leaves from 10 sprigs of thyme

1. To make the crumb mixture, place the almonds in a blender along with the breadcrumbs, cheese, lemon zest and thyme leaves, and whizz to a fine crumb.

2. Place each chicken breast between 2 pieces of cling film and, using a rolling pin, flatten evenly until about 1cm (½in) thick.

3. Break the eggs into a bowl and lightly beat, sprinkle the flour on to a plate and season with salt and pepper, then place the crumb mixture on another plate. Dip each chicken breast first in the flour, then in the egg and finally in the crumb. Place on a plate and put in the fridge. (The chicken can be left in the fridge for a few hours or overnight, if needed.)

4. When you are ready to cook, melt the butter in a large, non-stick pan over a medium heat and when it starts to bubble, add the chicken breasts and fry on one side for 3–4 minutes or until golden brown before turning over and frying for a further 2–3 minutes on the other side.

5. Remove from the pan and serve with a salad of rocket leaves lightly dressed in lemon juice and olive oil.

SPATCHCOCK CHICKEN WITH GREEK YOGHURT AND INDIAN SPICES

Spatchcocking is a great way to prepare chicken to be cooked in the oven, grilled or done on the barbecue, as it ensures the meat gets cooked more evenly. I tend to cook the recipe all together in the oven, but if you're using the grill or barbecue you will need less of the marinade. You don't have to stick exactly to the marinade recipe, try mixing and matching your favourite spices if you want. Moroccan flavours like cinnamon, cumin and apricots would also work well with the yoghurt.

SERVES 4

1 x 2kg (4lb 6oz) chicken, spatchcocked (see instructions on right or ask your butcher to do this)

300g (11oz) cherry tomatoes

FOR THE MARINADE

1 tsp fennel seeds

1 tsp fenugreek seeds

2 tsp black onion seeds

1 tsp ground turmeric

2 tsp dried oregano

2 tsp peeled and finely chopped garlic

2 tbsp peeled and finely chopped root ginger

250ml (9fl oz) plain Greek yoghurt, whisked until smooth

4 tbsp lime or lemon juice

2 tsp sesame oil

Salt and black pepper

1 tbsp extra-virgin olive oil or water (optional)

1. To make the marinade, first grind all the seeds for 1 minute in a spice grinder or coffee grinder, or using a pestle and mortar, then mix with the remaining ingredients, adding the oil or water to loosen the mixture if necessary.

2. To spatchcock the chicken place it, breast side down, on a chopping board and use scissors to cut through the flesh and bone along both sides of the backbone, in a strip about 5cm (2in) wide. Cut from tail to head end, completely removing the backbone.

3. Open out the bird, like opening a book, by gently pulling the two halves apart. Use a sharp knife to lightly score the top of the breastbone. Run your fingers along and under the sides of the breastbone and attached cartilage and pop them out. Spread the chicken out flat, then turn over and make a slit about 2.5cm (1in) long in the skin between the lower end of the breastbone and the leg, on each side. Stick the end of the leg on that side through the slit and repeat on the other side.

4. Spread the marinade all over the chicken, then place on a plate or baking tray, cover with cling film and refrigerate for at least 2 hours, or for up to 24 hours.

5. When ready to cook, preheat the oven to 200°C (400°F), Gas 6.

6. Remove the chicken from the fridge and place in a roasting tin, cover with foil and bake for 25 minutes. Add the cherry tomatoes to the tin and continue to cook for a further 15 minutes. Remove from the oven, then carve the chicken into slices and serve with the tomatoes and some boiled rice or a dressed salad.

BAKED CHICKEN WITH ARTICHOKE PURÉE AND BRAISED LENTILS

A lot of people seem to be put off by the idea of cooking lentils and pulses, perhaps because the soaking and cooking processes can be lengthy. But Puy lentils require less cooking than other types and will be done in under 30 minutes. They do need flavours added to them though, such as cumin and coriander, or rosemary, thyme and fennel seeds. However, don't season with salt until after the lentils are cooked or it will make the skins tough and unpleasant.

SERVES 4

4 tbsp olive oil

25g (1oz) butter

4 x 175g (6oz) boneless chicken breasts, with the skin on

Salt and black pepper

12 basil leaves, thinly sliced, to serve

FOR THE ARTICHOKE PURÉE

8 baby purple or 4–6 globe artichokes, outer leaves removed

100ml (3½fl oz) olive oil

25g (1oz) butter

125ml (4½fl oz) white wine

Juice of 1 lemon

75ml (3fl oz) double cream

FOR THE BRAISED LENTILS

2 tbsp olive oil

2 shallots, peeled and sliced

1 clove of garlic, peeled and crushed

200g (7oz) Puy lentils, rinsed

500ml (18fl oz) chicken stock (see pages 64–5)

2 sprigs of thyme, chopped

1. Preheat the oven to 200°C (400°F), Gas 6. Place a large, non-stick ovenproof pan over a high heat, add the olive oil and butter and season the chicken breasts with salt and pepper. When the butter has melted and starts to bubble, place the chicken in the pan, skin side down, and fry for 2 minutes or until browned, then turn over and place in the oven. Bake for 10 minutes or until cooked through, then remove, cover with foil and allow to rest for 4–5 minutes.

2. Meanwhile, prepare the artichokes. Place in a large saucepan, heads facing downwards, and add the olive oil, butter and wine. Cover the pan with a lid and set over a medium heat, then cook the artichokes for 15 minutes or until a sharp knife can be easily inserted into their centres.

3. When the artichokes are cooked, remove from the pan using a slotted spoon and cut in half. Place in a blender with the lemon juice and cream and purée until smooth, then season and set aside.

4. While the artichokes are cooking, prepare the lentils. Place another saucepan over a medium heat and add the olive oil, followed by the shallots and garlic. Sauté, without browning, for 2–3 minutes and then add the lentils. Mix together and pour in the stock. Bring to the boil, then reduce the heat and simmer for 25 minutes or until the lentils are tender. Stir in the thyme, season with salt and pepper and set aside.

5. To serve, place a smear of artichoke purée on one side of each plate, arrange the braised lentils in a line down the centre of the plate and lay the sliced chicken breast on top. Top with basil leaves, spoon over the juices from the pan and serve.

POACHED CHICKEN WITH A BROTH OF YOUNG VEGETABLES

I was introduced to this method of cooking chicken a few years ago and I love it because it keeps the breast meat so moist and tender. Poaching can take a little time but is worth it. When buying chicken, there are so many types to choose from, but the golden rule is to buy the best you can afford. I like Label Anglaise or the corn-fed variety.

SERVES 4

2 crowns of chicken
(about 575g/1lb 4oz each)

1 shallot, peeled and chopped

2 cloves of garlic, cut in half

2 sprigs of thyme

4 black peppercorns

Pinch of salt

1–2 tbsp olive oil

25g (1oz) butter

FOR THE VEGETABLE BROTH

25ml (1fl oz) olive oil

4 shallots, peeled and diced

100g (3½oz) pancetta, diced

1 carrot, peeled and sliced

4 baby turnips, cut in half

8 button mushrooms, sliced

2 radishes, sliced

1 clove of garlic, sliced

75ml (3fl oz) dry white wine

250ml (9fl oz) chicken stock
(reserved from step 2)

3 tbsp chopped chervil,
plus extra to garnish

50g (2oz) butter, diced

Salt and black pepper

1. To cook the chicken, place the crowns in a large saucepan and cover with cold water. Add the shallot, garlic, thyme, peppercorns and salt and bring to the boil, then reduce the heat and simmer for 3 minutes. Remove from the heat and allow to cool in the water.

2. Remove the chicken from the pan, place the pan back over a high heat and boil the stock to reduce the liquid by about half. Meanwhile, take a sharp knife and cut the chicken breasts from the crowns, cutting either side of the breastbone and slicing off the meat. Place the leftover bones in the boiling stock and set the breasts aside.

3. To make the broth, place another large pan over a medium heat and pour in the olive oil. Add the shallots and pancetta and fry for 2–3 minutes or until browned. Add the carrot, turnips, mushrooms and radishes and gently fry for a further 1–2 minutes, then add the garlic. Increase the heat, add the wine and boil for 1–2 minutes or until the volume of the liquid has reduced by half. Pass the chicken stock through a sieve and add to the pan, then reduce the heat and simmer for 3–4 minutes or until the vegetables are tender.

4. While the broth is cooking, place the olive oil and butter in a frying pan over a high heat. When the butter has melted and starts to bubble, sear the chicken breasts on both sides for 2 minutes or until browned, then remove from the heat and cut into slices.

5. Bring the broth to the boil and cook for a further 3–4 minutes or until the liquid has reduced to a thick glaze. Stir in the chopped chervil and diced butter and season with salt and pepper. Spoon the vegetables into bowls and arrange the sliced chicken on top, garnish with more chervil and serve.

BASIL CHICKEN WITH LIME

This is an Indian-style dish with clean and simple flavours. I've used chicken breast, but it also works nicely with chicken thighs or larger pieces of chicken – just marinate and cook them for longer than the recipe recommends.

SERVES 4

4 x 175g (6oz) skinless and boneless chicken breasts

75g (3oz) basil leaves

25g (1oz) coriander leaves

25g (1oz) mint leaves

1 green chilli, chopped

2 tbsp peeled and chopped root ginger

2 tbsp vegetable oil

2 tbsp plain yoghurt

Salt

TO SERVE

2 limes, cut into wedges

4 sprigs of watercress

1. Slice the chicken breasts into 4 pieces, place in a bowl and set aside.

2. Place the fresh herbs in a blender along with the chilli, ginger, vegetable oil and yoghurt, and purée to a smooth paste. Season with salt to taste and pour over the chicken pieces, stirring them in the marinade to coat evenly, then cover the bowl and leave in the fridge for 1 hour.

3. Preheat the oven to 200°C (400°F), Gas 6.

4. Remove from the fridge and lay the chicken pieces on a baking tray. Bake in the oven for 10–12 minutes or until cooked through, turning the chicken from time to time to ensure the pieces are evenly browned.

5. Remove from the oven and serve with lime wedges and sprigs of watercress.

'James has done it again! On his travels, he's absorbed ideas on flavour combinations, to bring us this array of yummy recipes to enjoy.'
MICHEL ROUX SNR

CHICKEN KIEV

This and prawn cocktail were about the only good things to come out of the 1970s. Chicken in a basket and over-cooked steak with baked potatoes and wrinkly peas have left me mentally scarred for life. But the Chicken Kiev began the ready-made food revolution and was Marks and Spencer's first ever ready meal back in 1976. It's the kind of retro food we shouldn't be without, and I wish more pubs and restaurants would put it back on their menus. I'm sure it would be a hit, just make sure to lose the basket...!

SERVES 4

4 x 175g (6oz) chicken breasts, French-trimmed (ask you butcher to do this)

100g (3½oz) plain flour

2 eggs

200g (7oz) fresh white breadcrumbs or dried breadcrumbs, such as Japanese panko

1.2 litres (2 pints) vegetable oil, for deep-frying

Salt and black pepper

FOR THE GARLIC BUTTER

6 cloves of garlic, peeled

150ml (5fl oz) milk

200g (7oz) butter, softened

25g (1oz) flat-leaf parsley, finely chopped

25g (1oz) chervil, finely chopped

4 COCKTAIL STICKS

1. To prepare the garlic butter, place the garlic in a small saucepan, cover with water and bring to the boil, then reduce the heat and simmer for 3 minutes. Drain the water away, then add the milk to the pan. Bring to the boil again, then reduce the heat and simmer for a further 3 minutes. Drain off the milk and reserve the garlic.

2. Crush the garlic and blend with the softened butter using a hand-held blender or electric beater. Transfer to a bowl, stir in the chopped herbs and season with salt and pepper. Place a piece of cling film 50cm (20in) long on a chopping board and spoon the butter on to the top part of the cling film. Roll the top part over and continue rolling to make a sausage shape about 20cm (8in) long and 2.5cm (1in) thick, then chill in the fridge for 1 hour to harden.

3. To prepare the chicken, insert a small sharp knife into the thick end of each breast. Poking the point of the knife into the chicken, cut a hole large enough for a 2.5 x 5cm (1 x 2in) piece of garlic butter to fit inside. Repeat with the other 3 breasts.

4. Remove the garlic butter from the fridge and slice into 4, then insert each piece into a chicken breast through the hole you have cut. 'Sew' up each hole using a cocktail stick.

5. To coat the chicken for deep-frying, first season the flour with salt and pepper and place on a plate. Break the eggs into a bowl and lightly beat, then place the breadcrumbs on another plate.

Continued...

6. Dip each chicken breast first in the flour, then in the beaten eggs and finally in the breadcrumbs. Then dip again in the egg but not the flour and again in the breadcrumbs to ensure the chicken is properly sealed and the butter doesn't leak out during cooking. Place the chicken breasts back in the fridge and leave, ideally for a few hours, before cooking.

7. If using a deep-fat fryer, heat the vegetable oil to 160°C (320°F). Alternatively, fill a deep, heavy-based saucepan to one-third with oil and use a sugar thermometer to check that it has reached the correct temperature. (Take great care if using a saucepan: always watch over it and never fill it beyond more than a third as the hot fat may bubble up when the chicken is added.)

8. Carefully lower the chicken breasts into the hot oil and deep-fry for 8–10 minutes or until golden brown. Remove from the oil and drain on kitchen paper then serve with a dressed green salad.

BRAISED CHICKEN THIGHS WITH FENNEL AND BAY LEAVES

I prefer the dark meat on chicken, for me it has the best flavour. With thighs you only get one bone, which can be easily removed before or after cooking if you wish. If, like me, you have a bay tree in the garden, you will have no shortage of leaves from it and this is a good dish to put them in. Another nice use for them is to pop the leaves on to the coals of a barbecue; they will impart some of their flavour on to whatever meat you're cooking.

SERVES 4

1–2 tbsp olive oil

12 chicken thighs, on the bone and with the skin on

1 onion, peeled and finely diced

1 fennel bulb, trimmed and finely diced

1 carrot, peeled and finely diced

1 clove of garlic, peeled and chopped

6 sprigs of thyme

2 bay leaves

Grated zest of 1 lemon

200ml (7fl oz) dry white wine, such as Sauvignon Blanc

500ml (18fl oz) chicken stock (see pages 64–5)

25g (1oz) butter

15g (½oz) flat-leaf parsley, chopped

Salt and black pepper

1. Preheat the oven 180°C (350°F), Gas 4.

2. Place a large, ovenproof pan over a high heat and add the olive oil. Season the chicken thighs with salt and pepper and place in the pan. Sear on both sides for 2 minutes or until browned, then transfer to a plate and set aside.

3. Add the onion, fennel and carrot to the pan and cook, without browning, in the chicken juices for 2–3 minutes. Add the garlic to the pan along with the thyme, bay leaves and lemon zest.

4. Place the chicken thighs back in the pan, pour in the wine and stock, stirring with a wooden spoon to release any vegetable pieces that may have stuck to the bottom of the pan. Bring to the boil and place in the oven to cook, uncovered, for 45 minutes.

5. When the chicken is cooked through, remove from the oven and allow to cool slightly before removing the thigh bones. To do this, hold each thigh in one hand and with the other pull the bone from one end and twist so that it works loose. Place the chicken in a serving dish and cover with foil to keep warm.

6. Place the pan back on the hob and boil for 2–3 minutes to reduce the sauce a little and thicken it. Add the butter and chopped parsley, remove the bay leaves and season well with salt and pepper, then pour over the chicken and serve.

POTATO AND DUCK CONFIT TERRINE WITH SWEET RED CABBAGE CHUTNEY

The word 'confit' means to preserve. It's a method that has been used for hundreds of years as a way to keep and store food for longer. The meat is first salted, then cooked in fat, and finally left in the fat until being eaten. Duck is often done like this and the French commonly confit goose, pork and turkey. I've even seen the method used for salmon and lamb. It allows you to use tougher cuts like the leg, because the process really tenderises the meat. So much so, that you should be able to eat it with a spoon when done properly.

SERVES 8–10

12 slices of Parma ham

2 tsp wholegrain mustard

500ml (18fl oz) double cream

Pinch of freshly grated nutmeg

750g (1lb 10oz) floury potatoes, such as Maris Piper, peeled and thinly sliced

500g (1lb 2oz) cooked duck legs (see page 83) skinned and meat removed from the bone

2 banana shallots, peeled and finely diced

4 tsp chopped flat-leaf parsley

75g (3oz) duck fat

Salt and black pepper

FOR THE CHUTNEY

150ml (5fl oz) rice vinegar

1 bay leaf

150g (5oz) dark brown sugar

300g (11oz) red cabbage, core removed and leaves finely shredded

TWO 1 LITRE (1¾ PINT) JARS
ONE 10 X 23CM (4 X 9IN)
TERRINE MOULD
ONE LARGE ROASTING TIN

1. To make the chutney, place a heavy-based saucepan over a high heat, pour in 150ml (5fl oz) of water and add the vinegar, bay leaf and sugar. Bring to the boil, then add the red cabbage, reduce the heat to a gentle simmer, cover with a lid and allow to cook for at least 30 minutes.

2. Just before the hour is up, remove the lid and bring back up to the boil, then boil until the liquid has almost evaporated. Remove from the heat and place in the jars (sterilised first in the dishwasher or by hand-washing them and heating them in the oven). Stored like this, the chutney will keep for up to 2 months.

3. Preheat the oven to 180°F (350°F), Gas 4.

4. Line the terrine mould with cling film, allowing extra to hang over the sides to cover the finished terrine. Next line the terrine with the Parma ham, allowing the slices to hang over the sides, then brush the ham with the mustard and then set aside.

5. Pour the cream into a small saucepan and bring to the boil, then add the grated nutmeg, season with salt and pepper and set aside. Layer the potatoes in the roasting tin, pouring the boiled cream over each layer and seasoning with salt and pepper, then bake in the oven for 35 minutes or until the potatoes are tender.

6. Remove from the oven and allow to cool, then cover with foil and a plate or tray weighted down with a couple of baked bean tins and chill in the fridge for 2 hours or until completely set.

Continued...

POTATO AND DUCK CONFIT TERRINE
WITH SWEET RED CABBAGE CHUTNEY *(cont.)*

7. Place the duck meat in a large bowl along with the shallots, parsley and the duck fat. Mix this together really well, then spread a couple of spoonfuls evenly over the bottom of the lined terrine mould. Remove the potatoes from the fridge and cut out a layer of potatoes to the same size as the bottom of the terrine or tin and place on top of the duck mixture, draining any excess cream.

8. Repeat this process until the terrine is full, finishing with a layer of duck. Fold over the overhanging ham, pressing it down, then fold over the cling film, again pressing down. Cut out a piece of card to fit the top of the terrine mould, cover the card with foil and place on top of the mould with a weight on top (the baked beans tins would be ideal), then place the terrine in the fridge to chill overnight.

9. Remove the weight from on top of the terrine and gently turn it out. Carefully peel away the cling film and slice the terrine. Place on individual plates, adding a spoonful of the chutney and serving with a handful of mixed leaves tossed in a little olive oil and lemon juice.

'Respect food – my mum and dad did.'
BRIAN TURNER CBE

HONEY-ROAST DUCK CONFIT WITH CRUSHED RATTE POTATOES

Ratte potatoes are hugely popular in France and can be found in every French supermarket. In Britain, with our increasing interest in new and different types of basic produce, we are finally starting to grow plenty of our own. What makes the ratte potato special is its skin, which has a lovely nutty taste, and the texture of the potato flesh, which is smooth and buttery. They're best boiled for salads, or boiled and crushed for dishes like this. They are also great simply roasted.

SERVES 4

4 duck legs
Leaves from 2–3 sprigs thyme
400g (14oz) duck fat
4 tbsp runny honey
Salt and black pepper

FOR THE CRUSHED POTATOES
400g (14oz) waxy potatoes, such as ratte, unpeeled
50g (2oz) butter
2 tbsp chopped chives

1. To make the duck confit, weigh the legs, place on a baking tray and sprinkle with 15g (½oz) of salt per 1kg (2lb 4oz). Scatter over thyme leaves, wrap in cling film and leave in the fridge overnight.

2. Remove the duck legs from the tray and place in a large, heavy-based saucepan. Cover with the duck fat and cook over a low heat for 1–1½ hours. Remove the pan from the heat and allow to cool, then remove the duck legs from the fat.

3. Preheat the oven to 180°C (350°F), Gas 4.

4. Scrape the fat from the duck legs, place in a roasting tin and smear over the honey. Roast the legs in the oven for about 20 minutes, spooning the honey glaze over the legs 2–3 times during cooking.

5. While the duck legs are roasting, place the potatoes in a large saucepan and bring to the boil, then reduce the heat and simmer for 15 minutes or until tender. Drain and then lightly crush with a fork. Stir in the butter and chopped chives and season with salt and pepper.

6. To serve, divide the potatoes between plates, placing the duck legs on the side and spooning over the juices from the roasting tin.

BANG BANG CHICKEN

This famous dish was originally a street food sold by vendors in the Sichuan region of China. Traditionally, the chicken would be tenderised with a wooden stick called a 'bon', hence it is also sometimes called Bon-bon chicken. It's not essential to whack your chicken, but if you've had a bad day then this is the dish to rid you of your anger.

SERVES 4

2 tbsp Sichuan peppercorns

2 cucumbers, peeled, deseeded and cut into matchsticks

Large pinch of salt

4 x 200g (7oz) skinless and boneless chicken breasts

3–4 tbsp groundnut oil

3–4 tbsp olive oil

2 large carrots, peeled and cut into matchsticks

4 spring onions, finely shredded, to serve

FOR THE SAUCE

130g (4½oz) chunky peanut butter or sesame seed paste

120ml (4¼fl oz) dark soy sauce

4 tbsp rice vinegar

2 tbsp sesame seed oil

3 tbsp granulated sugar

2 red chillies, finely diced

1. To toast the peppercorns, place them in a small saucepan over a medium heat and cook, shaking the pan from time to time, until they begin to darken. Remove from the pan and allow to cool, then crush with a rolling pin or using a pestle and mortar. Mix together in a bowl with the cucumber and a pinch of salt, then set aside.

2. In a separate bowl, whisk together all the ingredients for the sauce.

3. Using a sharp knife, cut the chicken breasts into thin slices and place in a bowl. Place a large wok or non-stick frying pan over a high heat and add the groundnut oil. When the oil is smoking hot, add the chicken pieces and sauté for 2–3 minutes or until cooked through, then transfer to a plate and set aside.

4. Clean the wok or pan and place back over the heat. Add the olive oil and sauté the carrot matchsticks for 1 minute, then remove and add to the chicken.

5. To serve, arrange the cucumber matchsticks on individual plates. Combine the chicken and carrots in the sauce and spoon on top of the cucumber, then top with the thinly sliced spring onions.

CHAPTER 4
RED MEAT

LAMB RACK AND BLACK

Black pudding is like Marmite – some love it, others loathe it. I personally love the stuff. It can be derived from sheep, goat, poultry or even horse, though it's pork that is used the most. The Germans have their famous Blutwurst, the Spanish have Morcilla and the French have their Boudin, but our version is definitely the nicest. In my opinion the best comes from Bury in Lancashire, and also Country Cork and Stornoway in Ireland. Go for one with bits in it, rather than one that is puréed and smooth on the inside.

SERVES 4

2 x 175–200g (6–7oz) racks of lamb, bones removed but with flap of skin and fat intact (ask your butcher to do this)

2 x 250–300g (9–11oz) black puddings (about 12cm/5in long and 2.5cm/1in wide), skin removed

2 tbsp vegetable oil

375ml (13fl oz) red wine

200–250ml (7–9fl oz) veal or beef stock

Salt and black pepper

1. Lay out 2 sheets of cling film, place one rack on top of each sheet and put a black pudding on the flap side of the lamb, close to the eye of the meat. Roll the joints up as tightly as possible and then wrap tightly in the cling film and place in the fridge for 30 minutes to rest.

2. Remove the racks from the fridge and carefully cut away the cling film, trying not to unwrap the meat as you do so, and then tie up the lamb at 1–2 cm (½–¾in) intervals with butcher's twine or string. (It's best to tie up each end first, see pages 106–7. This then prevents the whole joint from becoming misshapen during the tying process.) Chill in the fridge until needed. (They can be left in the fridge for a couple of days, if necessary.)

3. When you are ready to cook, preheat the oven to 200°C (400°F), Gas 6.

4. Place a roasting tin over a medium heat and pour in the vegetable oil. Season the racks with salt and pepper and place in the tin, searing on all sides for 1–2 minutes or until evenly browned, then place in the oven and roast until the meat is cooked to your liking. Roast for 8–10 minutes if you prefer your lamb to be pink; 15–18 minutes for medium; and 20–25 for well done. As with all roasts, once cooked it is important to let the meat rest for 4–5 minutes before carving.

Continued...

5. While the lamb is resting, pour away any excess fat from the roasting tin. Place the tin on the hob and add the red wine, then bring to the boil and reduce the cooking juices by three-quarters, stirring constantly to deglaze the tin. Pour in the stock and bring back up to the boil before straining through a sieve into a clean saucepan. Skim off any impurities from the top of the sauce and season with salt and pepper.

6. Remove the twine from the meat. The racks can each be cut into 6, allowing 3 thick slices per portion to ensure the best texture in both meats. Arrange on plates, pouring over the sauce and serving with Wilted Chard (see page 174) and Creamy Potato Mash (see page 179).

'Good food is just the first step towards a great meal.'
JAMES WINTER,
SATURDAY KITCHEN PRODUCER

LAMB CHOPS WITH ARTICHOKES, CAPERS AND TOMATOES

For too long now, many small artisan producers have been forced to close their doors after hundreds of years of trading because they can't compete with the supermarkets. When they shut up shop, generations of specialism and knowledge goes with them and there's little chance of it ever coming back. So a good butcher (in fact, any butcher) can be hard to find nowadays and if you are lucky enough to have one near you then you should give them all the support you can as their knowledge and produce is invaluable.

SERVES 6

150g (5oz) grilled artichoke from a jar, drained and rinsed

75g (3oz) capers from a jar, drained and rinsed

2 tbsp chopped basil leaves

2 tbsp chopped flat-leaf parsley

2–3 tbsp olive oil

12 lamb chops

Leaves from 2 Little Gem lettuces

Salt and black pepper

FOR THE SLOW-ROASTED TOMATOES

4 large tomatoes, cut in half

25ml (1fl oz) olive oil

2 cloves of garlic, peeled and sliced

1. Preheat the oven to 140°C (275°F), Gas 1.

2. First cook the tomatoes. Place the tomato halves cut side up in a ovenproof dish, drizzle with the olive oil, season with salt and pepper, sprinkle with the sliced garlic and bake in the oven for 1 hour.

3. Meanwhile, preheat the grill to high or prepare the barbecue.

4. Place the artichokes in a large bowl along with the capers, tomatoes and herbs, toss together and set aside.

5. Drizzle the olive oil over the chops, season with salt and pepper, place under the grill or on the barbecue and cook to your liking (2 minutes per side for rare, 4 minutes for medium and 6 minutes for well done), then remove from the heat and allow to rest for 2 minutes.

6. Add the Little Gem leaves to the bowl with the artichokes, toss together lightly and season with salt and pepper. Divide between plates, top with the chops and serve.

LAMB AND AUBERGINE BAKE

Many of you will recognise this as the Greek moussaka – lamb mince and aubergine layered up with a white sauce – but what you might not know is that there are also many variations around too. In Turkey, they do one with ingredients that are diced and mixed rather than layered, while in Bulgaria they use potatoes instead of aubergine. Whichever version you choose to make, it's delicious. It's one of those dishes that I can't help picking at when it's left out in the kitchen.

SERVES 4

3–4 tbsp olive oil

550g (1lb 3oz) minced lamb

1 large onion, peeled and diced

3 cloves of garlic,
peeled and crushed

1 tsp chopped oregano

2 sprigs of thyme

1 tsp ground cinnamon

1 x 400g can of chopped tomatoes

250ml (9fl oz) beef stock

2 aubergines, cut into
5mm (¼in) slices

150g (5oz) Gruyère cheese, grated

Salt and black pepper

FOR THE WHITE SAUCE

50g (2oz) butter

3 tbsp plain flour

700ml (1 pint 4fl oz) milk

½ tsp freshly grated nutmeg

2 egg yolks

**ONE 25 X 30CM (10 X 12IN)
OVENPROOF DISH**

1. Preheat the oven to 180°C (350°F), Gas 4. Place a heavy-based saucepan over a medium heat, add half the olive oil and the minced lamb and sauté for 3–4 minutes or until browned. Drain off excess liquid and add the onion, garlic, oregano, thyme and cinnamon. Sauté for 3–4 minutes or until the onion is browned, then add the chopped tomatoes and cook for a further 3 minutes. Pour in the stock, bring to the boil then reduce the heat and simmer for 20 minutes. Season with salt and pepper, remove from the heat and set aside.

2. Place a non-stick frying pan over a medium heat and drizzle in the remaining oil. Season the aubergine with salt and pepper and fry on each side for 2–3 minutes or until golden brown.

3. Meanwhile, make the white sauce. Melt the butter in a saucepan over a medium heat and when it bubbles add the flour and mix well. Carefully pour in the milk, stirring all the time to prevent lumps forming, then remove from the heat, season with salt, pepper and nutmeg, stir in the egg yolks and set aside.

4. Arrange a layer of aubergines in the bottom of the ovenproof dish, then some of the mince, alternating until the dish is full, finishing with a layer of aubergines.

5. Pour over the white sauce, spreading it out evenly, then sprinkle over the grated cheese and bake in the oven for about 1 hour or until cooked through and golden brown on top. Remove from the oven and allow to rest for 5 minutes before serving or it may burn your mouth. Serve with a green vegetable or with a simple salad of mixed dressed leaves.

BRAISED MEATBALLS WITH STAR ANISE AND TOMATO

A bit of a grown-up meatball with the addition of the anise, but kids will love them too as they have an aniseed flavour. I remember as a kid I loved those Sherbet Fountains, though I would normally empty away the sherbet and munch on the liquorice. The taste of this dish really takes me back. Anise is a versatile flavour and can go with pork, beef, chicken and even salmon.

SERVES 4

3 tbsp olive oil

1 shallot, peeled and finely diced

1 clove of garlic, peeled and crushed

400g (14oz) beef sirloin, diced and fat removed

300g (11oz) diced stewing beef

100g (3½oz) streaky bacon rashers

1 egg, beaten

30g (1¼oz) fresh white breadcrumbs

3 tbsp chopped flat-leaf parsley

Salt and black pepper

FOR THE SAUCE

4 tbsp olive oil

1 shallot, peeled and finely chopped

2 cloves of garlic, peeled and chopped

12 vine-ripened tomatoes, cut into quarters

1 tbsp light soft brown sugar

2 tbsp red wine vinegar

2 star anise

1. To make the sauce, place a heavy-based saucepan over a low heat and add the olive oil. Fry the shallot and garlic, without browning, for 5 minutes. Add the other ingredients and 100ml (3½fl oz) of water, and simmer very gently for 40 minutes.

2. Meanwhile, pour 1 tablespoon of olive oil into a small frying pan over a low heat, add the shallot and garlic and sauté, without browning, for 5–6 minutes, then allow to cool.

3. Place both types of beef and the bacon in a food processor, season well and pulse to a coarse consistency. (Try not to over-mix or it will look like sausage meat.) Remove from the machine and place in a large bowl, then stir in the egg, breadcrumbs and parsley, followed by the cooked shallots and garlic.

4. Using a large tablespoon, scoop a spoonful of the mixture into your hands, roll it into a ball and place on a plate or baking tray. Continue until all the mixture has been used up, then cover with cling film and leave in the fridge for at least 1 hour to firm up.

5. When you are ready to cook, preheat the oven to 200°C (400°F), Gas 6. Remove the star anise and purée the sauce, either in a food processor or using a hand-held blender, then place the star anise back into the sauce.

6. Place a large, ovenproof pan over a medium heat, add the rest of the olive oil, then fry the meatballs for 2–3 minutes or until lightly browned. Pour over the sauce, cover with foil and bake in the oven for 25 minutes. Serve straight from the oven with some freshly cooked pasta tossed in a little butter and/or a salad.

LEG OF LAMB STEAKS WITH HAZELNUT AND MINT PESTO

Lamb leg steaks are great for grilling, frying and cooking on the barbecue, but try not to overcook them as they're best eaten slightly pink. This recipe includes a twist on pesto, using mint as well as the usual basil. You can make the pesto in a machine but I think a pestle and mortar is better, if you have one. Sure, it takes longer and your arm will feel like you've done 100 press-ups, but it results in the best texture.

SERVES 4

2 tbsp olive oil

4 x 150g (5oz) leg of lamb steaks

Salt and black pepper

2 limes, cut into wedges, to serve

FOR THE HAZELNUT AND MINT PESTO

50ml (2fl oz) extra-virgin olive oil

25g (1oz) hazelnuts

1 clove of garlic, peeled

½ shallot, peeled and chopped

25g (1oz) fresh basil

25g (1oz) fresh mint

50g (2oz) fresh coconut flesh

Juice of 2 limes

1. First make the pesto. Place a griddle pan or frying pan over a high heat and add 20ml (¾fl oz) of the extra-virgin olive oil. Tip in the hazelnuts, garlic and shallot and sauté for 2–3 minutes or until the hazelnuts are lightly toasted, then place in a blender together with oil from the pan.

2. Add the basil, mint and coconut and quickly blitz to a chunky consistency, adding the remaining extra-virgin olive oil and lime juice to taste, then remove from the blender and set aside.

3. Place the griddle pan or frying pan back over a high heat, add the olive oil and season the lamb steaks with salt and pepper. When the pan is smoking hot, place the steaks in the pan and fry for 2 minutes, then, turning the steaks clockwise 90 degrees, cook for a further 2 minutes. Turn over and cook the lamb in the same way on the other side, this time brushing the steaks with some of the pesto after turning them clockwise.

4. Remove from the pan and place a lamb steak on each plate, then garnish with a spoonful of the pesto on the side and add a couple of wedges of fresh lime.

RIB-EYE STEAK WITH REDUCED RED WINE AND SHALLOT BUTTER

This is one of the easiest get-out-of-jail-free recipes you can have up your sleeve, ideal for when you need to knock up an interesting meal in just minutes. Making flavoured butter in advance and keeping it in the freezer means you've always got something ready to make a piece of meat more exciting. Flavoured butters also go nicely with fish, chicken, lamb or pork and can be flavoured with whatever vegetables, herbs or spices you like.

SERVES 4

4 x 225g (8oz) rib-eye steaks
1 tbsp olive oil
50g (2oz) butter
Salt and black pepper

FOR THE BUTTER
750ml (1 pint 6fl oz) red wine
4 tbsp redcurrant jelly
50ml (2fl oz) balsamic vinegar
6 shallots, peeled and finely diced
250g (9oz) butter, softened
1 tbsp chopped flat-leaf parsley

1. To make the butter, place the red wine, redcurrant jelly and balsamic vinegar in a large, heavy-based saucepan and bring to the boil. Add the shallots to the pan and keep boiling the wine mixture for about 30 minutes or until the liquid has reduced to a glaze.

2. Remove from the heat and allow to cool slightly before mixing it into the softened butter along with the chopped parsley. Season with salt and pepper and mix well together. Spoon on to a sheet of cling film, roll up into a sausage about 15cm (6in) long and place in the fridge for 1 hour to set.

3. To cook the steaks, place a large, non-stick frying pan over a high heat and season the beef well with salt and pepper. Add the olive oil and butter to the pan, allowing the butter to melt and start to bubble before adding the steaks.

4. Fry the steaks on one side for 3–4 minutes or until nicely browned, then turn over and cook on the other side for a further 2–3 minutes (or 3–4 minutes if you prefer your steak more well done).

5. Remove the steaks from the pan and place on individual plates, then take the butter from the fridge, remove the cling film, cut into 1cm (½in) slices and place 2 slices on top of each steak. Serve with chips (see page 46) or a crispy salad of Little Gem lettuce.

STEAK TERIYAKI WITH RADISH AND MUSTARD

Teriyaki brings a Japanese flavour to these otherwise fairly western ingredients. I recommend a really good 28-day-aged rump steak. As for the humble little radish, I rarely used it until I saw masses of them in the markets in Brittany. When I got home, I planted a few rows in the garden and within weeks I had loads. Freshly grown radishes are quite different from supermarket ones – they're full of moisture and the peppery flavour is much more intense and delicious.

SERVES 4

2 Little Gem lettuces

¼ small red onion, peeled, finely sliced and soaked in iced water for 15 minutes

10 radishes, finely sliced

2 tbsp vegetable oil

4 x 175g (6oz) rump steaks, about 2cm (¾in) thick

3 tbsp mirin

3 tbsp dark soy sauce (preferably Japanese)

3 tbsp sake

1 handful of pea shoots, to garnish

FOR THE MUSTARD DRESSING

1 tsp English mustard

2 tsp wholegrain mustard

½ tsp caster sugar

1 tsp red or white wine vinegar

1 tbsp rapeseed oil

Salt and black pepper

1. First make the mustard dressing by combining all the ingredients together in a bowl along with 1–2 tablespoons of water to taste. Mix well with a fork and set aside.

2. Break off the lettuce leaves and place on each plate with the curved side of the leaves facing up. Drain the sliced onion and mix together with the radishes in a bowl.

3. Place a large, non-stick wok or frying pan over a high heat and, once it is hot, pour in the vegetable oil then add the steaks and fry for 2–3 minutes or until browned.

4. Mix together the mirin, soy sauce and sake in a bowl and add to the steaks halfway through cooking. Coat the meat in the liquid as it reduces so that it takes on a glossy glaze, then remove from the heat, allowing it to rest for 3 minutes. Slice each steak on the diagonal and arrange on the lettuce leaves.

5. To serve, sprinkle over the sliced radishes and red onion, drizzle over the dressing and top with the pea shoots.

FILLET OF BEEF WITH SPINACH AND BÉARNAISE SAUCE

Steak and béarnaise is the best dish in the world if you ask me. It's real chefs' food and if ever this is on a menu, I always order it. Some people like to strain the shallots from the sauce, but I keep the bits in and think it tastes better for it. Béarnaise is based on a hollandaise sauce and is one of many classic variations that exist. Others include Sauce Choron, which is hollandaise with tomato purée, while Sauce Paloise has chopped mint added and is great with lamb.

SERVES 4

1 tbsp olive oil

50g (2oz) unsalted butter

4 x 150g (5oz) fillet steaks

150g (5oz) spinach,
any tough stalks removed

Sea salt and black pepper

FOR THE BÉARNAISE SAUCE

3 tbsp tarragon vinegar

50ml (2fl oz) white wine or water

1 tsp crushed white peppercorns

175g (6oz) unsalted butter

4 egg yolks

Juice of ½ lemon

Pinch of caster sugar

2 tbsp chopped tarragon

1. To make the Béarnaise sauce, pour the vinegar and wine or water into a saucepan, add the peppercorns and bring to the boil, simmering rapidly until the liquid has reduced by half. Strain out the peppercorns and set the vinegar mixture aside.

2. In a separate pan set over a low heat, melt the butter until it separates, then strain and keep the clear butter, discarding the milk solids left in the sieve.

3. Place the egg yolks and the cooled vinegar mixture in a bowl set over a saucepan of simmering water and whisk together. Slowly add the clarified butter, continuing to whisk until all the butter has been combined, then remove the bowl from the pan, season with salt and pepper and add the lemon juice, sugar and tarragon. Mix together then set aside while you cook the steaks.

4. Place a heavy-based frying pan over a medium heat, add the olive oil and half the butter. When the butter has melted and starts to bubble, add the steaks and fry for about 4 minutes on each side for rare and 2–3 minutes longer if you prefer your steaks more well done. Season the steaks with salt and pepper before turning over to cook on the other side.

5. Meanwhile, cook the spinach. Melt the remaining butter in a saucepan over a medium heat and add the spinach, cover with a lid and cook for about 1 minute or until it wilts, then drain and divide between plates.

6. To serve, place a steak on top of the spinach on each plate and spoon over some of the Béarnaise sauce.

THE BEST BEEF BURGERS
IN THE WORLD

What can I say? These burgers speak for themselves and certainly beat anything you'll
ever get from a drive-through.

SERVES 4

*1–2 tbsp olive oil, plus
extra for oiling*

2 shallots, peeled and finely chopped

*700g (1½lb) tail of beef fillet
or top-quality minced beef
(with minimum fat)*

4 tbsp chopped gherkins

2 tbsp double cream

½ tsp Dijon mustard

Splash of Worcestershire sauce

Salt and black pepper

TO SERVE

4 burger buns, sliced in half

50g (2oz) mixed salad leaves

4 tsp mayonnaise (optional)

1. Pour the olive oil into a small frying pan set over a medium
heat and sauté the shallots for 1–2 minutes to take off the rawness,
then allow to cool.

2. Mince the beef fillet by passing it through the fine plate of a
mincer and into a bowl. If using minced beef, place it straight
in the bowl. Add the shallots, gherkins, cream, mustard and
Worcestershire sauce, beat well together and season with salt
and pepper.

3. Rubbing a little oil on your hands, shape the mixture into
4 even-sized patties, place on a plate and set aside for 10 minutes.

4. Meanwhile, preheat the grill to high.

5. Place the burgers under the grill and cook on each side for
3–4 minutes for rare to medium, 5–6 minutes for well done, then
remove from the grill and allow to rest.

6. While the burgers are resting, toast the bun halves on both
sides, then place some salad leaves on 4 of the bun halves, adding
a little mayonnaise first if you liked, and top with the burgers
and remaining bun halves. Serve on their own or with chips
(see page 46).

ESCALOPE OF ROSE VEAL WITH CARAMELISED LEMON

Veal has had a lot of bad press over the years but much has changed in the way it's now produced. I come from a farming background, so I know that if you drink milk you really have no argument not to eat veal. However, much of the breeding for veal goes on in Europe where the standards are still nowhere near as strict they are in the UK. So look for 'rose veal', which is produced in the UK, and you can be confident that the animals have been looked after in the best way possible.

SERVES 4

700g (1½lb) cushion of rose veal

2 eggs

100g (3½oz) plain flour

Butter, for cooking

4 large lemons, cut in half

Salt and black pepper

FOR THE HERB CRUST

200g (7oz) loaf of white bread crust removed and the bread torn into chunks

Peel of 4 lemons (removed with a potato peeler)

50g (2oz) onions, peeled and roughly chopped

2 cloves of garlic, peeled

8 sprigs of thyme

6 tbsp olive oil

1. Preheat the oven to 140°C (275°F), Gas 1.

2. First make the herb crust. Place the bread on a baking tray and add the lemon peel, onions, garlic and thyme. Drizzle with the olive oil and bake in the oven for 30–40 minutes to dry the bread out.

3. Remove from the oven and allow to cool, then transfer to a food processor and whizz into a fine crumb.

4. Cut the cushion of veal into 8 slices, allowing 2 per portion and making sure you cut through the grain of the muscle of meat and not along it. Placing each slice between 2 pieces of cling film and using a rolling pin, flatten the escalopes evenly until they are each about 1cm (½cm) thick.

5. Break the eggs into a bowl and beat lightly, scatter the flour on a plate, seasoning with salt and pepper, and add the breadcrumbs to another plate. Then dip each escalope first in the flour, then in the egg and finally in the crumbs, place on a large plate and leave to chill in the fridge for 1 hour or overnight if needed.

6. Melt the butter in a large, non-stick frying pan over a high heat and once it starts to bubble, add the escalopes and fry on each side for 1–2 minutes or until golden brown. Depending on the

Continued...

size of your pan, you may have to cook the meat in 3–4 batches. Place the cooked escalopes on a plate in a warm oven while you finish frying the rest.

7. At the same time add the lemons halves to the pan, cut side down, and leave that way up in the pan while you cook the meat. That way the lemons with brown well on the cut side.

8. Serve the escalopes on individual plates with 2 caramelised lemon halves on the side and some of the butter from the pan spooned over the top.

THE CLASSIC BEEF WELLINGTON

This is a true kitchen classic and will test any cook to hold their nerve. It's said to be named after the Duke of Wellington, who loved beef, truffles and mushrooms. (Well, so do I, but I'm a long way from getting a dish named after me!) Whether it is true or not, these classic flavours never fail to impress. One of the Wellington's real advantages is that it can be made well ahead of time. Do make sure to include the pancakes as they will help to soak up some of the beef juices and stop the puff pastry from becoming soggy.

SERVES 4–6

1–2 tbsp vegetable oil

500g (1lb 2oz) beef fillet (middle section), fat removed

25g (1oz) butter

100g (3½oz) portobello mushrooms, finely chopped

4 slices of Parma ham

75g (3oz) smooth chicken liver pâté

1 x 375g packet of ready-rolled all-butter puff pastry

1 egg yolk, beaten

FOR THE PANCAKES

3 eggs

6 tbsp plain flour

150ml (5fl oz) milk

40g (1½oz) butter

FOR THE GRAVY

500ml (18fl oz) chicken stock (see pages 64–5)

150ml (5fl oz) red wine

Dash of balsamic vinegar

3 tbsp softened butter

25CM (10IN) NON-STICK FRYING PAN

1. First make the pancakes. Place the eggs and flour in a bowl and whisk together. Gradually add the milk and whisk the batter to a consistency that will coat the back of a spoon. Heat the 25cm (10in) frying pan until really hot, add a quarter of the butter and, when it has melted, pour in a quarter of the batter to thinly coat the base of the pan. When the batter has set, flip over and cook the other side. Tip out on to a plate lined with greaseproof paper, then repeat, making 4 pancakes in total and layering each between sheets of greaseproof paper.

2. Place a separate non-stick frying pan over a medium heat and add the vegetable oil. Season the beef fillet with pepper and then place in the pan and sear for 1 minute on each side. Remove from the heat and set aside.

3. Melt the butter in another frying pan over a high heat, then add the chopped mushrooms and fry for 3–4 minutes or until all the excess moisture has evaporated. Season well with salt and pepper and allow to cool slightly, then purée in a food processor or using a hand-held blender.

4. Place the pancakes flat on a work surface, overlapping slightly. Spread with the puréed mushrooms, then top with the Parma ham. Spread the pâté over the top of the beef and then place it on the ham. Fold up to enclose the beef.

Continued...

5. Roll out the pastry on a lightly floured work surface until it forms a square 33cm (13in) wide and 5mm (¼in) thick. Place the pancake-wrapped-beef in the centre, brush the surrounding pastry with beaten egg yolk, then fold up and turn the edges of the pastry towards each other on one side.

6. Place the beef parcel, seam side down, on to a baking sheet and brush with more of the egg yolk, then chill in the fridge for 30 minutes.

7. Meanwhile, preheat the oven to 200°C (400°F), Gas 6.

8. Remove the beef from the fridge and brush again with the remaining egg yolk. Bake in the oven for 30 minutes or until golden, then remove from the oven and allow to rest for 5 minutes.

9. To make the gravy, pour the stock and red wine into a saucepan and boil to reduce by a third, then whisk in the balsamic vinegar and butter. Season with salt and pepper, pour over the sliced beef Wellington and serve.

'Cooking might be seen as an art by some, but chefs should never forget that stomachs need to be filled.'
MICHEL ROUX JNR

SHOULDER OF LAMB WITH ROSEMARY AND LEMON AND MINTED POTATOES

Any part of an animal that does a lot of work usually tastes the best but also requires the most amount of cooking. The shoulder is one of those parts, and when slow-roasted it's definitely one of the best cuts of lamb to eat. You can buy it boned or whole – it makes no difference really, apart from being easier to serve if the bone has already been removed. This dish is best placed in the centre of the table in Henry VIII banquet style so that everyone can just dive in.

SERVES 4

2kg (4lb 4oz) boneless shoulder of lamb, rolled and tied (ask your butcher to do this or see method on pages 106–7)

Grated zest and juice of 3 lemons (retain the squeezed halves)

Leaves from 2 large sprigs of rosemary

75g (3oz) peeled and chopped root ginger

3 cloves of garlic, peeled and crushed

150ml (5fl oz) rapeseed oil

Sea salt and black pepper

FOR THE MINTED POTATOES

2kg (4lb 6oz) Jersey Royal potatoes, unpeeled

75g (3oz) mint leaves

75g (3oz) unsalted butter

1. Place the lamb in a roasting tin with the lemon halves underneath for support.

2. Place the rosemary in a food processor along with the ginger, garlic, lemon zest and juice and rapeseed oil, and blitz for 1 minute. Season the lamb with salt and pepper and then massage the rosemary and lemon mix into the meat. Set aside to marinate for about 20 minutes.

3. Meanwhile, preheat the oven to 140°C (275°F), Gas 1.

4. Pour 150ml (5fl oz) of water into the roasting tin with the lamb, cover the whole tin with foil and cook in the oven for 45 minutes. After the 45 minutes, turn the temperature up to 180°C (350°F), Gas 4, remove the foil and cook for 20 minutes to brown the lamb, basting the joint occasionally with the juices.

5. Meanwhile, cook the potatoes. Place the potatoes in a large, heavy-based saucepan, cover with cold water and bring to the boil, then reduce the heat, add the mint leaves and simmer for 20 minutes or until the potatoes are tender. Remove from the heat and drain, then season with salt and pepper, stir in most of the butter and place in a large, warmed serving dish with the remaining butter dotted on top.

6. Remove the lamb from the oven and allow to rest for 10 minutes before cutting off the string. Carve the meat and divide between plates, drizzle over the cooking juices and serve with the potatoes.

CHAPTER 5
PORK

TYING A JOINT FOR ROASTING

The reason for tying a joint is to help it keep its shape while cooking. A loin of pork is the best cut with which to try this, and a saddle of lamb also works nicely, but in fact you can use this technique for any type of meat or fish: either just tied, or first stuffed and then tied.

1. Place the joint of pork, fat side up, on a chopping board and loop some butcher's twine or string around one end of the joint, leaving about 10cm (4in) of twine hanging from the end.

2. Pull out more twine and twist it to make a loop, then slip this loop over the other end of the loin and slide it along towards the end with the initial loop.

3. Tighten well, without cutting into the meat, and adjust the loop to ensure the knot remains in the centre of the joint.

YOU WILL NEED

* *A loin of pork or saddle of lamb, with fat*
* *Butcher's twine or string*

  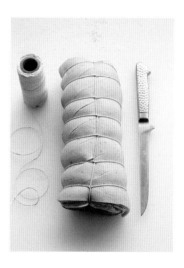

4. Continue to do this, twisting it into loops, slipping each one over the opposite end and sliding along to sit at 2cm (¾in) intervals, until the entire piece is firmly tied.

5. Turn the meat over and cut the twine, leaving a piece about 7.5cm (3in) longer than the joint, then weave this piece of twine though the loops.

6. Finally tie the two ends of the twine together to secure the joint, and the meat is ready to roast.

RUSTIC PORK PÂTÉ

The secret to good pâté is the quality of the ingredients that go into it. Remember that there is no such thing as cheap good food. Yes, pâtés are generally considered inexpensive but it doesn't mean that the ingredients should be cheap. You can make this recipe a little different by adding diced game, hazelnuts or pistachio nuts. If you want, you could line the bowl with streaky bacon and, when cooked, turn it out and serve at the table as a whole.

SERVES 6–8

350g (12oz) pork shoulder, diced

1 tbsp whole black peppercorns

12 juniper berries

450g (1lb) streaky bacon rashers, diced

300g (11oz) smoked streaky bacon rashers, diced

250g (9oz) chicken livers, cut into 1cm (½in) cubes

2 cloves of garlic, peeled and crushed

1 tsp chopped thyme

Pinch of ground mace

1 tsp salt

50ml (2fl oz) brandy

100ml (3½fl oz) double cream

ONE 1.75 LITRE (3 PINT) OVENPROOF DISH

1. Place the diced pork in a food processor and blend until it is finely chopped, then remove and place in a large bowl.

2. Crush the peppercorns and juniper berries using a pestle and mortar, or by placing them in a sealed plastic bag and crushing them with a rolling pin, and add to the pork along with the bacon lardons and diced chicken livers.

3. Add the garlic, thyme, mace and salt. Pour in the brandy and cream and mix all the ingredients well, then cover the bowl and leave in the fridge for 1 hour.

4. Meanwhile, preheat the oven 150°C (300°F), Gas 2.

5. Transfer the mixture into the ovenproof dish and pack it down well. Place the dish in a large roasting tin half filled with hot water and bake in the oven for 1½ hours.

6. Remove from the oven and allow to cool before covering with foil and a plate that fits just inside the dish. Put a weight on top of the plate (a couple of tins of baked beans would do) and place the pâté in the fridge to chill overnight.

7. Remove the pâté from the fridge 40 minutes before serving to allow it to come to room temperature, then carefully turn out on to a large plate. Scrap off the excess jelly from around the edges and serve in slices with bread or toast and a few gherkins or some tomato or apple chutney (see page 112).

ROAST LOIN OF PORK WITH GRILLED APPLES

My favourite type of pork for this recipe is Gloustershire Old Spot, which has an excellent fat-to-meat ratio and, when roasted, the skin crisps up nicely. Chard is from the same family as beetroot, but unlike the beets, where you eat the base, with chard you eat the leaves and stems. A popular ingredient in the Med, at last we are catching on, and as such it can now be found all year round. It comes in many colours – I grow yellow, red and green – and it is very simple to cook.

SERVES 4

1.5kg (3lb 4oz) boneless, rolled pork loin (ask your butcher to do this or see method on pages 106–7)

2 onions, unpeeled and roughly chopped

375ml (13fl oz) red wine

200–250ml (7–9fl oz) chicken stock (see pages 64–5)

Salt and black pepper

FOR THE GRILLED APPLES
2 green eating apples
50g (2oz) caster sugar

1. Preheat the oven to 180°C (350°F), Gas 4. Score the pork skin horizontally with a sharp knife, at intervals of about 2.5cm (1in), and season with salt and pepper. Place the onions in a roasting tin and lay the pork on top, then roast in the oven for 45 minutes, basting occasionally with the cooking juices. Reduce the temperature to 170°C (325°F), Gas 3, and cook for a further 40 minutes, then remove from the oven and allow to rest for 15 minutes.

2. While the pork is cooking, peel the apples, cut them in half widthways and remove the core. Place a non-stick frying pan over a medium heat, sprinkle the apple halves with the sugar and place, presentation side down, into the pan. Cook for 2–3 minutes to allow to caramelise, then turn over and repeat the process. If the apples seem to be drying out, add 2–3 tablespoons of water, allowing it to evaporate. Remove from the heat and set aside.

3. While the pork is resting, remove the onions and pour away any excess fat from the roasting tin. Place the tin on the hob and add the red wine, then bring to the boil and reduce the cooking juices by three-quarters, stirring constantly to deglaze the tin. Pour in the stock and bring back up to the boil before straining through a sieve into a clean saucepan. Skim off any impurities from the top of the sauce and season with salt and pepper.

4. Carve the pork and the crackling, allowing 2 slices per person, then top each portion with a caramelised apple half and serve with the gravy, Creamy Potato Mash and the Wilted Chard with Hazelnuts (see pages 179 and 174).

SHOULDER OF PORK WITH BOULANGÈRE POTATOES

Boulangère is a classic French potato dish. The name translates as 'baker' and the dish is so-called because after the village bakeries had finished baking all their bread for the day, the locals would bring their pots of potatoes to cook in the residue heat of the bread ovens. Some of the original ovens are still in use now, hundreds of years later. They are wood-fired and often the grapevines from the vineyards are used to fuel them.

SERVES 6–8

1.5kg (3lb 4oz) pork shoulder

2–3 tbsp olive oil

3 large white onions

6 large baking potatoes

750ml (1 pint 6fl oz) chicken stock (see pages 64–5)

Coarse sea salt and black pepper

1. Preheat the oven to 170°C (325°F), Gas 3.

2. Place the pork in a roasting tin, skin side up, and rub with the olive oil and plenty of salt and pepper, then roast in the oven for 3 hours, basting from time to time with the cooking juices.

3. While the pork is cooking, peel and thinly slice the onions and the potatoes and set aside.

4. Remove the pork from the oven, lifting it out of the tin, then place the potatoes in the tin along with the onions, season with salt and pepper and cover with the stock.

5. Place the tin on the lowest shelf of the oven and put the pork on the shelf directly above the potatoes so that the fat from the meat drips into the tin, and cook for a further 2 hours.

6. Remove the pork from the oven 5 minutes before you take out the potatoes, to allow it to rest. Carve the meat into thick slices and cut the crackling into pieces, place on individual plates and serve with a big spoonful of the potatoes on the side and some buttered French beans.

PORK BURGERS WITH APPLE CHUTNEY AND RAREBIT

The secret to a great burger is normally in getting the right ratio of prime meat to fat: too much fat and it masks the taste of the meat you are using, too little and the burger can end up very dry. However, a good solution is to use pork as it doesn't tend to dry out as much as beef, so you can get away with less fat. Be careful if you're cooking these on a barbecue as they really cause the flames to flare up.

SERVES 4

600g (1lb 5oz) minced pork
(with minimum fat)

2 egg yolks

25g (1oz) flat-leaf parsley,
finely chopped

2 tbsp olive oil

Salt and black pepper

FOR THE APPLE CHUTNEY

100g (3½oz) demerara sugar

75g (3oz) sultanas

6 eating apples

2 shallots, peeled and chopped into
1cm (½in) dice

1 tbsp peeled and chopped
root ginger

1 red chilli, finely chopped

2 tomatoes, chopped into
1cm (½in) dice

1 tsp salt

150ml (5fl oz) malt vinegar

1. First make the apple chutney. Place a heavy-based frying pan over a medium–high heat and add the sugar. Once the sugar starts to caramelise, stir until a nice golden colour is achieved, then add the sultanas and cook for 1 minute or until they start to puff up.

2. Peel and core the apples and chop into 1cm (½in) dice, then add these to the pan along with the shallots, ginger, chilli and tomatoes. Mix well, then pour in the vinegar and add the salt. Bring to the boil and cook for 15–20 minutes or until the apples start to soften but before they turn to a purée. Remove from the heat and allow to cool before pouring into the jar (sterilised first in a dishwasher or by hand-washing it and heating it in the oven). Stored like this, the chutney will keep for up to 6 months.

3. Prepare the rarebit by placing the milk in a pan and warming through, without boiling, over a gentle heat. Add the grated cheese to the pan, allowing it to dissolve in the milk, then add the flour and cook for 1 minute, stirring with a wooden spoon. Remove from the heat and allow to cool, then beat together the egg and yolk and add to the pan along with the mustard, breadcrumbs and a dash of Worcestershire and Tabasco sauce. Season with salt and pepper and place in the fridge.

Continued...

FOR THE RAREBIT

75ml (3fl oz) milk

325g (11½oz) mature Cheddar, grated

30g (1¼oz) plain flour

1 egg

1 egg yolk

½ tsp mustard powder, or to taste

25g (1oz) fresh white breadcrumbs

Dash of Worcestershire sauce

Dash of Tabasco sauce

Salt and black pepper

ONE 1 LITRE (1¾ PINT) PRESERVING JAR

4. Place the pork in a large bowl and add the egg yolks and parsley, then season with salt and pepper and mix well. Divide the mixture into 4 and shape into burgers, dipping your hands into a bowl of cold water to stop the mixture sticking to your fingers.

5. Place a non stick pan over a medium heat and pour in the olive oil. Add the pork burgers and fry on each for 4–5 minutes or until golden brown.

6. While the pork burgers are cooking, preheat the grill to medium–high.

7. Remove the rarebit from the fridge and shape into flat patties 1cm (½in) thick and the same size as the pork burgers.

8. Place the burgers on the grill tray, top each with a piece of rarebit and place under the grill for 2–3 minutes to brown on top. Remove from the grill and serve with the apple chutney on the side and some mixed salad leaves tossed in a little Sherry Vinaigrette (see page 152).

'A really great British meal on a cold winter's day, with all the trimmings, is one of life's greatest pleasures.'
CYRUS TODIWALA OBE

CHINESE PORK AND GINGER DUMPLINGS

Certain ingredients have the power to change the way I think about cooking. Yuzu juice is one of these ingredients and I just can't get enough of the stuff. A yuzu looks like a small grapefruit with a flavour and smell somewhere between a mandarin and a lime. We sell it in the deli but you can also get it online and from specialist Asian food stores. I've got no doubt it will be in supermarkets soon. Yuzu juice goes brilliantly with Chinese dumplings. I've used pork but you can use chicken instead, or fish such as crab or salmon.

SERVES 4
(MAKES 24 DUMPLINGS)

24 wonton wrappers

1 egg white, beaten

3–4 tbsp sunflower oil

Large handful of chive lengths, to serve

FOR THE STUFFING

300g (11oz) minced pork (with minimum fat)

1 egg white

1 shallot, peeled and very finely chopped

2 tsp peeled and grated root ginger

Dash of Thai fish sauce

FOR THE SAUCE

6 tbsp dark soy sauce (preferably tamari)

4 tbsp sesame oil

3 tbsp yuzu juice

1 tbsp chopped coriander

1. To make the stuffing, place the pork, egg white, shallot, ginger and dash of fish sauce in a blender and blitz to a rough paste – trying not to over-mix as it should be a reasonably coarse texture rather than a purée.

2. Next lay the wonton wrappers on your work surface and place a spoonful of the pork mixture on one half of each of the wrappers. Brush the edges of the wrappers with a little of the beaten egg white, then fold over and press the edges to seal. Using your fingers, make small pleats along the edges – it should look like a little bag with the edges crimped together at the top.

3. Pour half the sunflower oil into a large, non-stick frying pan or wok set over a high heat and fry half the dumplings for 2 minutes to lightly brown them, then remove from the pan and fry the second half in the remaining oil. Once they are browned, add around 75ml (3fl oz) of water, cover with a lid, reduce the heat and steam for 5–6 minutes. (Depending on the size of your pan or wok, you may need to steam the dumplings in two batches as well.)

4. Meanwhile, combine all the ingredients for the sauce in a bowl. To serve, lay some chives on each plate then remove the dumplings from the pan, placing 6 on each plate, and serve the sauce alongside.

PORK LOIN WITH BRANDY AND MUSHROOM SAUCE AND FRIES

This pork is served with a delicious Brandy and mushroom sauce. It can be made in minutes but it is important when using strong liqueurs like Brandy or brandy to flame off the alcohol, otherwise the flavour tends to overpower everything else, especially the delicate mushrooms. It's essential to use double cream too, as single cream will split when boiled, and don't even think about swapping it for crème fraîche either – it just won't work!

SERVES 4

1–2 tbsp olive oil

50g (2oz) butter

750g (1lb 10oz) pork loin, cut into 5mm (¼in) slices

2 shallots, peeled and sliced

75g (3oz) baby onions, peeled

150g (5oz) pancetta, diced

150g (5oz) wild mushrooms (such as chanterelle, cep, trompette, girolle or oyster)

50ml (2fl oz) brandy

100ml (3½fl oz) chicken stock (see pages 64–5)

100ml (3½fl oz) double cream

2 tsp wholegrain mustard

3 tbsp chopped flat-leaf parsley

Salt and black pepper

FOR THE FRIES

1.2 litres (2 pints) vegetable oil, for deep-frying

4 large baking potatoes peeled and cut into matchsticks

1. Place a non-stick frying pan over a medium heat and add 1 tablespoon of the olive oil and half the butter. Season the pork slices and fry on each side for 3 minutes or until browned, then put on a baking tray and keep warm in a low oven.

2. Place the pan back on the hob, over a high heat, adding a little more oil, if necessary, and the remaining butter, and tip in the shallots, onions and pancetta. Fry for 1–2 minutes or until the onions are softened and the pancetta is crispy, then add the mushrooms and cook for a further minute.

3. Pour in the brandy and carefully set alight, allowing the alcohol to flambé until the flame goes out. Pour in the stock and simmer for 1–2 minutes, then stir in the cream and mustard, season with salt and pepper and set aside.

4. If using a deep-fat fryer, heat the vegetable oil to 190°C (375°F). Alternatively, fill a deep, heavy-based saucepan to one-third with oil and use a sugar thermometer to check the temperature. (Take great care if using a saucepan: always watch over it and never fill it more than a third as the hot fat may bubble up when the potatoes are added.)

5. Fry the potatoes in the hot oil for 3–4 minutes or until golden brown and cooked through. Remove with a slotted spoon and drain on kitchen paper, then season with salt and pepper.

6. Reheat the sauce gently, stirring in the parsley, then divide the pork slices between plates, pour over the sauce and serve with the straw fries on the side.

CHAPTER 6
PASTA & GRAINS

MAKING PASTA

Yes, I know this needs a lot of egg yolks, but it is the best, and I do mean the best, pasta recipe I have learnt over the years. It comes from one of the great Italian cooks in the UK – I thought he was mad when he started to make it like this, but it works and when you eat the finished pasta you realise what a difference it makes. Do buy a pasta machine; they're quite cheap. Once you master the simple technique of tagliatelle you can move on to ravioli, and before long you'll be opening your own restaurant.

1. Place all the ingredients in a food processor and pulse to form a dough, trying not to over-mix. Alternatively, sift the flours into a bowl and beat the egg and egg yolks together in a separate bowl. Make a well in the centre of the flour and pour in the beaten egg and the olive oil, then mix together, adding a little more flour if the mixture seems too sticky.

2. Tip out on to a chopping board or work surface lightly dusted with flour and work to a dough with your hands, then wrap with cling film and leave in the fridge for 30 minutes to rest.

3. Cut the pasta dough in half, lightly dust each section with flour and feed through a pasta machine on its thickest setting. Roll the pasta into thin sheets, reducing the roller width each time you feed the pasta through the machine until it is on its thinnest setting.

YOU WILL NEED

* *200g (7oz) '00' pasta flour, plus extra for dusting*
* *50g (2oz) fine semolina flour, plus extra for dusting the pasta strips*
* *1 egg and 6 egg yolks*
* *1 tbsp olive oil*
* *A pasta machine*

4. Place the roller cutters on the pasta machine and feed the pasta through to cut it into strips – thin ribbons or wider strips, whatever you prefer.

5. Once made, use the pasta strips immediately or dry them for about 2 hours by suspending over a clean broom handle propped up between two chairs.

6. When dry to the touch, place the pasta strips on a baking tray and dust in semolina flour to prevent them from sticking together. The pasta can then be coiled into nests and stored in a plastic bag or airtight container for 2–3 days.

TAGLIATELLE ALLA BOLOGNESE

This classic ragù sauce shouldn't really be served with spaghetti, as is so often done in the UK. Make it with tagliatelle and you'll see how much better it tastes. It's also very important to mix the sauce properly with the pasta, so that the flavours and tastes are combined in every mouthful. Please don't do the norm and stick a bowl of plain pasta in front of people with just a blob of sauce on top.

SERVES 4

300g (11oz) fresh or dried tagliatelle

FOR THE BOLOGNESE SAUCE

1–2 tbsp olive oil

100g (3½oz) pancetta or dry-cured streaky bacon rashers, chopped into lardons

25g (1oz) butter

1 large onion, peeled and finely chopped

1 carrot, peeled and finely chopped

600g (1lb 5oz) minced beef (preferably Aberdeen Angus)

200ml (7fl oz) milk

300ml (11fl oz) red wine

1 bay leaf

450ml (16fl oz) beef stock

1 x 400g can of chopped tomatoes

Salt and black pepper

1. Place a large, heavy-based saucepan over a high heat, add the olive oil and the pancetta and fry for 2 minutes or until browned, then remove with a slotted spoon, drain on kitchen paper and set aside.

2. Add the butter and tip in the onion and the carrot, then reduce the heat and cook for 5 minutes to soften. Increase the heat and add the beef, cooking for 5–6 minutes or until browned.

3. Pour in the milk, red wine and bay leaf, then bring to the boil and cook for 5 minutes before adding the stock, tomatoes and pancetta. Bring back up to the boil, then reduce the heat to low, cover with a lid and simmer for 1½ hours.

4. Shortly before the sauce has finished cooking, prepare the pasta. Cook the tagliatelle according to the instructions on the packet, or boil in salted water for 2–3 minutes if using fresh, homemade pasta.

5. To finish the sauce, season well with salt and pepper and serve with the cooked tagliatelle.

CLASSIC LASAGNE

In Italy, classic dishes often vary a great deal between the north and south of the country. Lasagne is one such dish – in the south they use much more of the ragù sauce, while the version they have in the north is closer to what we know, with plenty of white sauce topping. The name of the dish is thought to come from the Greek word for a chamber pot (nice!) – the Romans borrowed the word to refer to their cooking pots.

SERVES 4

14–16 sheets of fresh or dried lasagne

3 x 125g (4½oz) balls of mozzarella cheese, sliced

100g (3½oz) Parmesan, freshly grated

Salt and black pepper

FOR THE MEAT SAUCE

4 tbsp olive oil

1 onion, peeled and finely chopped

2 sticks of celery, trimmed and finely chopped

2 carrots, peeled and finely grated

3 cloves of garlic, peeled and finely chopped

Leaves from 1 sprig of rosemary or thyme, chopped

700g (1½lb) minced beef (preferably Black Angus)

350g (12oz) minced pork (with minimum fat)

750ml (1 pint 6fl oz) red wine

Continued...

1. First make the meat sauce. Place a large, heavy-based saucepan over a medium heat and pour in the olive oil. Add the onion, celery and carrots and fry for 4–5 minutes or until softened and lightly browned. Add the garlic and rosemary or thyme and cook for a further 2 minutes.

2. Tip in the minced beef and pork, increase the heat and fry for 3–4 minutes or until the liquid from the meat has evaporated. Pour in three-quarters of the wine and bring to the boil, then reduce the heat and simmer for 30 minutes or until the wine has been absorbed.

3. Add the tomatoes and pour in the stock, bring back up to the boil, then reduce the heat to low and cook, uncovered, for 1 hour, adding a little water or more stock if the mixture looks too dry. Season with salt and pepper and remove from the heat.

4. Meanwhile, make the white sauce. Pour the milk into a large, non-stick saucepan, add the onion, bay leaves and nutmeg and bring to the boil, then remove from the heat. Melt the butter in a separate saucepan over a low heat, then stir in the flour and cook for 2 minutes. Add the milk, a little at a time, to the flour mixture, mixing it well between additions. until all the milk has been absorbed. Remove from the heat and set aside.

5. Preheat the oven to 180°C (350°F), Gas 4, and start assembling the lasagne.

Continued...

2 x 400g cans of chopped tomatoes

300ml (11fl oz) beef stock

FOR THE WHITE SAUCE

1 litre (1¾ pints) milk

½ onion, peeled

2 bay leaves

Pinch of freshly grated nutmeg

50g (2oz) butter

50g (2oz) plain flour

ONE 30CM (12IN) SQUARE OVENPROOF DISH

6. If using dried pasta that needs pre-cooking, first blanch the sheets for 3 minutes in a large saucepan of boiling salted water, then drain.

7. Spread a third of the meat sauce in the bottom of the ovenproof dish and arrange a third of the sheets of pasta over the top. Spread a third of the white sauce over this, along with some mozzarella slices and a sprinkling of Parmesan and black pepper. Repeat this step twice, using up all the ingredients and finishing with a layer of mozzarella and Parmesan.

8. Place in the oven and bake for 30–40 minutes or until golden brown and bubbling. Serve immediately with a crisp green salad.

'Simple things done well are better than complicated things done badly.'
GALTON BLACKISTON

MOROCCAN SPICED COUSCOUS WITH HONEY AND ALMONDS

Couscous is made by rolling and shaping moist semolina wheat and then coating it in fine wheat flour, so whereas bulgur wheat is natural, couscous is manufactured. This is a really quick and instant salad that works on its own or alongside fish or meat. You can add fruit like apricots or pomegranate seeds, which go brilliantly with the Moroccan spices.

SERVES 4–6
VEGETARIAN (IF MADE WITH VEGETABLE STOCK)

25g (1oz) butter

2 shallots, peeled and finely diced

½ tsp ground ginger

½ tsp ground coriander

1 tsp ground cumin

1 cinnamon stick

100g (3½oz) flaked almonds

100ml (3½fl oz) runny honey

½ red chilli, deseeded (optional) and diced

1 clove of garlic, peeled and finely diced

4 tomatoes, deseeded and diced

175g (6oz) couscous

500ml (18fl oz) vegetable or chicken stock (see pages 64–5) or water

50g (2oz) chopped coriander

Grated zest and juice of 1 lemon

Salt and black pepper

1. Melt the butter in a large frying pan over a medium heat and when it starts to bubble, add the shallots, ground spices and the cinnamon stick and fry for 1 minute just to soften the shallots. Add the almonds and keep mixing for 3–4 minutes to toast the almonds. Then add the honey, chilli, garlic and tomatoes, bring to the boil, then reduce the heat and simmer for 2 minutes. Pour into a large serving bowl.

2. Add the couscous, then bring the stock or water to the boil and carefully pour over the couscous, stirring it in with a spoon. Cover the bowl and leave for 5 minutes.

3. Once the couscous has absorbed all the liquid, fluff up with a fork to break up any large pieces, then stir in the chopped coriander and lemon zest and juice, season with salt and pepper and serve.

RAVIOLI WITH MINCED LAMB AND TOMATO

Once you've mastered the homemade pasta on pages 118–19, this is phase two. When making ravioli, try to not leave too much air inside the pasta parcels as this will cause them to burst. They do freeze well but for me they're best cooked from fresh. If you don't want to cook them immediately, place in the fridge on a tray of semolina until you're ready.

**SERVES 4
(MAKES ABOUT 16 RAVIOLI)**

*1 x quantity of pasta dough
(see page 118)*
Extra flour, for dusting
2 eggs, beaten
Extra-virgin olive oil, for drizzling

FOR THE FILLING
1–2 tbsp olive oil
*½ onion, peeled
and finely chopped*
1 garlic clove, peeled and crushed
375g (13oz) minced lamb
4 tbsp chopped mint
50g (2oz) mascarpone cheese
Salt and black pepper

1. First make the filling. Place a non-stick frying pan over a medium heat and pour in the olive oil. Add the onion and garlic and gently fry for 2–3 minutes or until softened. Tip in the minced lamb, season well with salt and pepper and cook for 10–12 minutes or until the lamb is cooked through and nicely browned.

2. Stir in the chopped mint, then remove from the heat, draining off any excess liquid or oil from the pan, and allow to cool. When the mixture has cooled, add the mascarpone and set aside.

3. To make the tomato sauce, place a heavy-based saucepan over a medium heat, then add the olive oil and the tomatoes and sauté for 2–3 minutes. Add the shallots and garlic and cook for a further 5–6 minutes.

4. Sprinkle over the sugar and some salt and pepper and cook for a further couple of minutes, then remove from the heat and add the basil leaves. Pour the mixture into a blender, or use a hand-held blender, and blitz to a form a coarse-textured sauce, then pour back into the pan and keep warm while you prepare the ravioli.

Continued...

FOR THE TOMATO SAUCE

50ml (2fl oz) olive oil

500g (1lb 2oz) ripe tomatoes, chopped

2 shallots, peeled and chopped

2 cloves of garlic, peeled and crushed

Pinch of caster sugar

3 large basil leaves, chopped

PASTA MACHINE
ONE 4CM (1½IN) DIAMETER PASTRY CUTTER AND ONE 5CM (2IN) CUTTER

5. Cut the pasta dough in half, lightly dust each section with flour and feed the pasta through the machine on its thickest setting. Roll the pasta into thin sheets, reducing the roller width each time you feed the pasta through the machine until it is on its thinnest setting.

6. Lay the sheets out on a work surface lightly dusted with flour and, using the pastry cutters, cut half the pasta into discs 3cm (1½in) in diameter and the other half into discs 5cm (2in) in diameter. Spoon the filling on to the smaller discs, leaving a small gap around the edge of each circle, brush the edges with some of the beaten eggs and top each with one of the larger discs, pinching the discs together to seal.

7. Bring a large saucepan of salted water to the boil, then drop in the ravioli, allowing them to cook for 1–2 minutes. Carefully remove from the water with a slotted spoon and divide between plates. Drizzle with a little olive oil, pour over the tomato sauce and serve.

POTATO GNOCCHI WITH HERBS AND SAFFRON

Gnocchi can be made from potatoes and flour, like this, or there's also a version that uses a choux-pastry base. This potato gnocchi is so quick to knock up and can be served like pasta with a variety of sauces, or included in soups to bulk them out a bit.

SERVES 4

50ml (2fl oz) white wine

2 good pinches of saffron

1kg (2lb 3oz) baked potatoes, cut in half

300g (11oz) plain flour, plus extra for dusting

3 egg yolks, beaten

75g (3oz) Parmesan, freshly grated, plus a few extra shavings to serve

25g (1oz) chervil, chopped

50g (2oz) unsalted butter

Salt and black pepper

1. Pour the wine into a saucepan set over a low heat, add the saffron and allow to infuse for 2–3 minutes, then remove from the heat and set aside.

2. Scrape the cooked potato flesh into a large bowl and mash with a fork, seasoning with salt and pepper. Pour in the saffron-infused wine and stir in the flour, then gradually add the egg yolks, mixing them in a little at a time, followed by the cheese and the chervil. Cover the bowl and allow to rest in the fridge for 30 minutes.

3. Remove the gnocchi mixture from the fridge and place on a lightly floured surface, rolling it into a long sausage shape about 2.5cm (1in) in diameter. Cut the dough into 2.5cm (1in) slices, then, using your fingers or a fork, mould each slice into a small, rugby-ball shape.

4. Bring a large saucepan of salted water to the boil, then plunge the gnocchi in and allow to cook for 1–2 minutes. Remove from the pan and place in a bowl of ice-cold water to cool, then drain.

5. Melt the butter in a large, non-stick frying pan over a medium heat, then add the gnocchi and fry for 2–3 minutes or until golden brown. Season with salt and pepper and serve with a few Parmesan shavings sprinkled over the top and some buttered spinach or green beans.

TABBOULEH WITH CHARRED LEMONS

This Middle-Eastern dish is always made with bulgur wheat, not couscous, and varies so much from region to region. The main thing is not to use too much of the bulgur wheat compared to the rest of the ingredients. The Lebanese use lots more parsley than wheat in theirs and I think the dish really benefits from it. So try to include plenty of full-flavoured ingredients, such as herbs and charred lemons, to give the salad a stronger taste.

SERVES 4–6

VEGETARIAN

(IF USING VEGETABLE STOCK)

175g (6oz) bulgur wheat

700ml (1 pint 4fl oz) vegetable or chicken stock (see pages 64–5)

6 tbsp extra-virgin olive oil

2 lemons, cut in half

2 small red onions, peeled and finely chopped

100g (3½oz) pistachio nuts, shelled and chopped

Grated zest and juice of 2 lemons

8 tbsp chopped flat-leaf parsley

8 tbsp chopped coriander

5 tbsp chopped mint

Salt and black pepper

1. Place the bulgur wheat in a large saucepan, pour in the stock and bring to the boil, then reduce the heat to low, cover the pan with a lid and simmer for 15–20 minutes. When the bulgur wheat is tender, remove from the heat and allow to stand, with the lid still on the pan, for 10 minutes.

2. Place a non-stick frying pan over a high heat and when it is hot, add 1 tablespoon of the olive oil. Add the lemon halves, cut side down, and fry for 2–3 minutes or until golden brown, then remove from the pan.

3. Add the remaining ingredients to the bulgur wheat and mix well. Season to taste with salt and pepper and serve with the charred lemon halves on the side. (If serving the tabbouleh cold, it's best to add the fresh herbs shortly before serving or they will discolour.)

ROAST PUMPKIN RISOTTO WITH FRIED SAGE LEAVES

This can be made either with pumpkin or butternut squash. I love to grow my own squash and pumpkin, which do well in the compost heap at the end of my garden. Once you've made the purée, you can place it in a freezer bag and freeze it until you need it. I like to serve this dish with frisée lettuce as the leaves have a sharp taste that works with the creaminess of the risotto.

SERVES 4

400g (14oz) peeled and deseeded pumpkin flesh

2–3 tbsp olive oil

25g (1oz) butter

1 shallot, peeled and finely chopped

1 clove of garlic, peeled and finely chopped

175g (6oz) Arborio rice

100ml (3½fl oz) white wine

700ml (1 pint 4fl oz) vegetable stock

75g (3oz) Parmesan cheese

50g (2oz) mascarpone cheese

1 tbsp finely chopped chives

Salt and black pepper

TO SERVE

1 tbsp olive oil

Large handful of sage leaves

Leaves from 1 frisée lettuce heart

2 tbsp extra-virgin olive oil

Juice of 1 lemon

1. Preheat the oven to 200°C (400°F), Gas 6.

2. Cut the pumpkin flesh into 2.5cm (1in) chunks and place on a baking tray. Drizzle with the olive oil and season with salt and pepper, then cover with foil and bake in the oven for 30 minutes or until the pumpkin feels soft to the point of a knife. Remove from the oven, blitz to a purée in a blender, then transfer to a bowl and set aside.

3. Melt the butter in a large, heavy-based saucepan over a medium heat, add the shallot and garlic and sauté, without browning, for 2 minutes. Stir in the rice, then pour in the white wine and half the stock. Bring to the boil, then reduce the heat and simmer gently for 13–15 minutes. As the rice absorbs the liquid, keep adding more stock until the rice is just cooked.

4. Add the puréed pumpkin to the rice and mix well – at this point it should be like rice pudding in consistency. Stir in the Parmesan and mascarpone, then add the chopped chives and season well with salt and pepper.

5. To prepare the sage leaves, place a frying pan over a low–medium heat, add the tablespoon of olive oil and gently fry the leaves, without browning them, for 1–2 minutes on each side.

6. Dress the salad leaves in the extra-virgin olive oil and a little of the lemon juice, to taste, stirring the remainder of the lemon juice into the risotto. Spoon the risotto on to each plate, top with some dressed salad leaves and fried sage leaves and serve.

POLENTA WITH WILD MUSHROOMS AND PARMESAN

Polenta is made of maize and, while it is thought of as Italian, it was originally from America and didn't reach Europe until the seventeenth century. However, it was the Italians who developed it into the dish that it is today; previously it was simply eaten like porridge. Although it is often served wet with shaved Parmesan, it can also be served like this: cooled and then griddled or pan-fried. It also works well on the barbecue. It needs to be accompanied by a sauce or something liquid, else the whole meal can be too dry.

SERVES 4

75g (3oz) butter,
plus extra for greasing

600ml (1 pint) vegetable stock

125g (4½oz) polenta

Leaves from 2 sprigs of thyme

75g (3oz) Parmesan cheese,
freshly grated

2 shallots, peeled and finely chopped

1 clove of garlic, peeled
and finely chopped

300g (11oz) mixed wild mushrooms
(such as chanterelle, cep,
trompette, girolle or oyster)

2–3 tbsp extra-virgin olive oil,
plus extra to serve

2 tsp chopped flat-leaf parsley

50g (2oz) Parmesan, shaved
with a potato peeler

Salt and black pepper

1. Grease a baking tray with a little butter, then pour the stock into a large saucepan and heat to a simmer. Tip the polenta into the pan, stirring all the time, then add the thyme leaves and continue stirring for 5–6 minutes over a low heat. Add 50g (2oz) of the butter and the cheese and season with salt and pepper. Pour on to the greased baking tray and allow to cool.

2. Melt the remaining butter in a frying pan over a high heat and when it begins to bubble, add the shallots and garlic and cook for 30 seconds. Tip in the mushrooms and fry for 2–3 minutes.

3. Meanwhile, place a griddle pan, or a heavy-based frying pan, over a high heat. Cut the polenta up into 8 squares, drizzle with the olive oil and chargrill in the pan for 1–2 minutes on each side or until browned.

4. Remove from the heat and place 2 pieces of polenta on each plate. Add the parsley to the mushrooms and season with salt and pepper, serving a portion of these on the side, with a drizzle of olive oil and sprinkling of Parmesan shavings over the top.

CLASSIC PILAF

There are so many varieties of pilaf, from the Italian and Greek styles, to the Afghan version that uses more of a broth-type sauce, to the Persian variation that has meat and vegetables added. You can alter the colour by adjusting the spices or by adding well-cooked diced onions, which give it a brown appearance.

SERVES 4–6
VEGETARIAN

200g (7oz) basmati rice
25ml (1fl oz) olive oil
½ tsp cumin seeds
1 cinnamon stick
¼ tsp ground turmeric
2 cloves
4 cardamom pods
1 bay leaf
1 white onion, peeled and thinly sliced
25g (1oz) flaked almonds
25g (1oz) sultanas
25g (1oz) butter
Good pinch of saffron
Good pinch of salt
25g (1oz) chopped pistachios
4 tbsp chopped coriander

1. First place the rice in a colander and rinse under cold water until the liquid runs clear, then set aside to drain.

2. Pour the olive oil into a non-stick pan over a low heat, add the cumin seeds, cinnamon stick, turmeric, cloves, cardamom and bay leaf and fry for 20–30 seconds or until the spices become fragrant. Add the onion and fry for 6–8 minutes or until golden brown. Tip in the almonds and sultanas and cook for a further minute, then add the butter.

3. Add the drained rice, stirring well to coat it in the oil and spices, then pour in 400ml (14fl oz) of water. Add the saffron and salt and bring to the boil, then reduce the heat to low, cover with a lid and simmer for 7–8 minutes or until the rice is tender but still has a slight bite to it.

4. Add the chopped pistachios and coriander and stir well, fluffing the rice with a fork as you mix. Set aside for 4–5 minutes, uncovered, to allow any excess water to evaporate, then serve.

LINGUINI WITH SEA BASS, MUSSELS AND TOMATO

I first made this while on my holiday in my motor home (yes, motor home, not caravan!). I wanted a quick meal for some mates that were coming over and this was the end product. They all enjoyed it so I hope you do too.

SERVES 4

450g (1lb) live mussels

200g (7oz) fresh or dried egg linguini

50ml (2fl oz) extra-virgin olive oil, plus extra for drizzling

2 cloves of garlic, peeled and finely sliced

1 x 400g can of chopped tomatoes (preferably Italian)

450g (1lb) sea bass fillets, pin bones and skin removed and sliced into strips

275g (10oz) brown shrimps or chopped prawns

20g (¾oz) flat-leaf parsley, chopped

Salt and black pepper

1. Wash the mussels in a colander to remove any dirt or grit. Pick through them, removing any stringy 'beard' from the shells. If any of the mussels are slightly open, tap them on the work surface to see if they close (which means they're still alive) and discard any that remain open.

2. Cook the linguini according to the instructions on the packet, or boil in salted water for 2–3 minutes if using fresh, homemade pasta. Remove from the heat and drain in a colander.

3. While the pasta is cooking, place a large, heavy-based saucepan over a medium heat, add half the olive oil and the garlic and cook, without browning, for 1 minute, then add the canned tomatoes. Bring to the boil, reduce the heat and simmer for 2 minutes, then add the mussels, place a lid on the pan and cook for a further 3–4 minutes in the sauce or until the mussels start to open.

4. Meanwhile, pour the remaining olive oil into a large, non-stick frying pan set over a high heat and add the sea bass. Fry in the hot oil for about 3 minutes, then add the shrimps or chopped prawns and the mussels and stir well. Tip in the drained pasta and continue cooking the sauce for 1–2 minutes, then add the chopped parsley and season well with salt and pepper.

5. To serve, divide between bowls, discarding any mussels that remain closed, and drizzle with more olive oil.

CHAPTER 7
VEGETARIAN

POACHING AN EGG

The poached egg is one of the true tests of a good chef. This and the boiled egg (and of course I should include the omelette here too, as I've seen many chefs cook that!). The good thing about poached eggs is that, once you've cooked them, you can blanch them in ice cold water and then keep in the fridge until needed. To reheat, just plunge into simmering water for 1 minute and you will have perfect poached eggs every time.

1. Place a large saucepan of water to heat on the hob, then crack each egg into a small pot, such as an espresso cup, being careful not to break the yolk.

2. Once the water is boiling, reduce to a simmer and add 1 tablespoon of white wine vinegar.

3. Whisk the water around the pan to create a whirlpool, then carefully tip the egg into the centre of the whirling water.

YOU WILL NEED

* Eggs
* White wine vinegar
* Iced water

4. Allow the egg to simmer in the water for 2 minutes, during which time it will start to come together and the white will set.

5. Lift the egg from the boiling water with a slotted spoon and plunge straight into a bowl of iced water. Repeat the process with the rest of the eggs. Once all the eggs have been poached, neaten the edges with a sharp knife and then place the eggs back into a bowl of clean cold water.

6. At this stage you could place the bowl in the fridge, leaving the eggs there overnight if needed. To reheat the eggs, bring a saucepan of fresh water to a gentle simmer, then drop the eggs into the water. Simmer for 1 minute, then remove using a slotted spoon, drain on kitchen paper and serve.

BEETROOT AND SHALLOT TARTES TATIN WITH GOAT'S CHEESE

These tarts may look complicated but they're very easy to make and a nice savoury alternative to the classic apple tarte Tatin that most people think of as a dessert. This version was on my restaurant menu once, served with a truffle honey dressing, and it was a huge success. If you want to try the dressing, it's just a small amount of truffle oil mixed with really good-quality runny honey.

MAKES 4 TARTS
VEGETARIAN

2 soft goat's cheeses, such as Perroche
50g (2oz) watercress
4 tbsp extra-virgin olive oil
1 tbsp balsamic vinegar

FOR THE TARTS
100g (3½oz) caster sugar
50g (2oz) butter
200g (7oz) cooked small beetroot (not in vinegar), peeled
200g (7oz) small shallots, peeled and kept whole
1 clove of garlic, peeled and finely chopped
250g (9oz) ready-rolled all-butter puff pastry
Salt and black pepper

FOUR 10CM (4IN) DIAMETER
NON-STICK TART TINS

1. Preheat the oven to 200°C (400°F), Gas 6.

2. First make the tartes Tatin. Place a non-stick saucepan over a medium–high heat, add the sugar and allow to caramelise. Add the butter and mix together with the caramelised sugar, then remove from the heat and pour the mixture into the tart tins and set aside.

3. Cut the beetroot into small wedges and divide these and the shallots between the tins, inserting them into the caramel until each tin is packed full. Place little pieces of the chopped garlic on to each of the tarts and season well with salt and pepper.

4. Cut the pre-rolled puff pastry into 4 discs, each about 2cm (¾in) larger in diameter than one of the tart tins. Place a disc of pastry on top of each tin, tucking in the edges down the sides to seal in the shallots and beetroot. Bake in the oven for 15 minutes or until the pastry is golden brown.

5. Meanwhile, tip the cheeses into a bowl and mix to a paste using a spoon, then dress the watercress in the olive oil and vinegar and set aside.

6. To serve, tip the tarts out of the tins while still hot and place on each plate, topping with some of the dressed leaves and a spoonful of the creamed cheese.

ONION BHAJIS WITH TOMATO SAUCE

This Indian street food must be one of the biggest-selling dishes in curry houses all around the UK. Normally eaten as a snack along with poppadoms, bhajis can also be served as a nice dish in their own right. You can spice up the sauce with chilli if you wish, or to save time just serve the bhajis with some chutney from a jar. Great with peppery watercress.

SERVES 4
(MAKES 12–16 BHAJIS)
VEGETARIAN

1.2 litres (2 pints) vegetable oil

1 egg, beaten

½ tsp ground cumin

Pinch of cayenne pepper

300g (11oz) chickpea flour

2 onions, peeled and finely sliced

Salt and black pepper

FOR THE TOMATO SAUCE

2 tbsp olive oil

2 shallots, peeled and finely diced

2 sprigs of thyme

2 cloves garlic, peeled and crushed

8 tomatoes, skinned, deseeded and chopped (see method on page 12)

1 tsp tomato purée

150ml (5fl oz) white wine

1. To make the tomato sauce, place a heavy-based saucepan over a medium heat and pour in the olive oil. Add the shallots, thyme and garlic and fry, without browning, for 1 minute, then add the tomatoes and cook for 3–4 minutes. Add the purée and cook for a further 2–3 minutes. Pour in the wine, bring to the boil, then reduce the heat and simmer over a low heat for 10 minutes.

2. Remove from the heat and purée in a blender. Season with salt and pepper, then pour back into the pan and keep warm over a low heat while you cook the bhajis.

3. If using a deep-fat fryer, heat the vegetable oil to 180°C (350°F). Alternatively, fill a deep, heavy-based saucepan one-third with oil and use a sugar thermometer to check the temperature. (Take great care if using a saucepan: always watch over it and never fill it more than a third as the hot fat may bubble up when the bhajis are added.)

4. In a bowl, combine the egg, cumin, cayenne pepper and flour to form a paste, seasoning with salt and pepper and adding a little water to loosen it if needed. Dip a heaped tablespoon of the onions in the batter mixture, then drop into the hot fat and cook for 2–3 minutes or until golden brown.

5. Repeat with the rest of the mixture, frying in 1–2 batches. Remove the cooked bhajis with a slotted spoon and drain on kitchen paper before placing in a warmed serving dish. The filled dish can be kept in the oven, preheated to 200°C (400°F), Gas 6, while you cook the remaining bhajis, although they taste best straight from the pan. Serve with the tomato sauce.

GLAZED FOLDED OMELETTE WITH BROAD BEANS

What I haven't learnt about omelettes from the 200 or so Saturday Kitchen omelette challenges isn't worth knowing. This is a dish I do at home (without the clock running!) using broad beans from my garden. You can use frozen ones but they do need blanching and peeling – it is fiddly, but if you have kids, get them to do it for some pocket money.

SERVES 4
VEGETARIAN

4–5 tbsp olive oil, plus extra for oiling

12 eggs

150ml (5fl oz) double cream

25g (1oz) chives, chopped

150g (5oz) frozen broad beans, blanched and peeled (see method on page 12)

100g (3½oz) Cheddar cheese, grated

Salt and black pepper

1. Preheat the grill to high and lightly oil a baking sheet.

2. Crack the eggs into a large bowl and season with salt and pepper. Pour in the cream and whisk until combined, then add the chopped chives.

3. Place a large, non-stick frying pan over a medium–high heat and drizzle in a little of the olive oil. Pour in a quarter of the egg mixture, spreading it around the pan and allowing it to cook for 1 minute or until it starts to set.

4. Sprinkle over some of the beans then, with a palette knife, fold the omelette in two, remove from the heat and slide on to the oiled baking sheet. Repeat for the remaining 3 omelettes, then sprinkle with the cheese and place under the grill for 2–3 minutes or until glazed golden brown on top.

5. Remove from tray and place on individual plates, serving with a fresh green salad and new potatoes.

COURGETTES AND SHALLOTS IN BLACK BEAN SAUCE

Chinese flavours work well to quickly enhance vegetables. You could of course make your own black bean sauce, but the ready-made jars are so convenient that I bet you wouldn't, even if I put the recipe here. The sauce is delicious and very popular – we sell masses of it in the Deli – and this recipe is really easy, so give it a go.

SERVES 4
VEGETARIAN

2 tbsp rapeseed oil

6 banana shallots, peeled and sliced lengthways

6 courgettes, topped and tailed and cut into ribbons

150ml (5fl oz) black bean sauce

2 tbsp chopped coriander leaves

Salt and black pepper

1. Place a large, non-stick frying pan over a medium heat and pour in the rapeseed oil. Add the shallots and sauté for 2–3 minutes or until they are lightly browned, then add the courgettes, toss together and cook for a further 2–3 minutes.

2. Pour in the black bean sauce and cook for 3–4 minutes more, then remove from the heat. Add the chopped coriander, season to taste with salt and pepper, and serve with boiled rice or stir-fried noodles.

BRAISED FENNEL WITH BREADCRUMBS AND RICOTTA

Fennel is an under-used vegetable – it always seems to be the only one left on the supermarket shelf on a Saturday night. What a shame, when it has one of the most distinctive flavours of any vegetable. It can be braised like this, or thinly sliced and served in salads (such as the recipe on page 53). Don't let the fennel dry out while cooking; keep topping up the water in the dish if it's running low. This recipe makes a great side dish, a delicious tapas-style snack or can be eaten cold.

SERVES 4
VEGETARIAN

2 fennel bulbs, trimmed and cut into quarters lengthways

200ml (7fl oz) white wine

Leaves of 2 sprigs of thyme

2 cloves of garlic, peeled and crushed

25g (1oz) caster sugar

100g (3½oz) fresh white breadcrumbs

150g (5oz) ricotta cheese

Salt and black pepper

1. Preheat the oven to 170°C (325°F), Gas 3.

2. Place the fennel quarters in a roasting tin, pour over the wine and 150ml (5fl oz) of water, then add the thyme and garlic. Season with salt and pepper, cover with foil and bake in the oven for 25 minutes.

3. Remove from the oven and sprinkle over the sugar, then allow to cool. Drain the cooking juices, reserving a little of them, and set the fennel aside, still in the roasting tin.

4. Combine the breadcrumbs and ricotta in a bowl, season with salt and pepper and scatter over the fennel, adding a little of the cooking juices if the mixture looks too dry. Place back in the oven and cook for 10–15 minutes or until browned, then serve immediately.

BAKED ONION TARTS WITH WILD ROCKET

Vegetarians will love these tarts, as they're packed full of flavour. All-butter puff pastry is essential, as that is where lots of the flavour comes from. The tarts can be made up beforehand and just cooked when you want them.

MAKES 4 TARTS
VEGETARIAN

100ml (3½fl oz) olive oil, plus extra for oiling

2 large red onions, peeled and cut in half

75ml (3fl oz) balsamic vinegar

2 sprigs of thyme

1 clove of garlic, peeled and chopped

200g (7oz) ready-rolled all-butter puff pastry

1 egg yolk, beaten

2 tsp wholegrain mustard

4 x 50g (2oz) slices of goat's cheese

Salt and black pepper

TO SERVE
30ml (1¼fl oz) extra-virgin olive oil

50g (2oz) wild rocket

ONE 15CM (6IN) DIAMETER PASTRY CUTTER

1. Preheat the oven to 200°C (400°F), Gas 6, and oil a baking tray with olive oil. Place the onion halves, cut side up, in a ovenproof dish, drizzle with the olive oil and balsamic vinegar and add the thyme and garlic. Season with salt and pepper, cover with foil and bake in the oven for 35–40 minutes or until soft when pricked with a sharp knife, then remove from the oven and allow to cool.

2. While the onions are cooling, roll out the puff pastry to around 3–4mm (⅛in) thick and cut into 4 discs each 15cm (6in) wide, place on the oiled baking tray and brush with the beaten egg yolk.

3. Spoon the mustard on to the discs, leaving a 1cm (½in) gap around the edge, and place a slice of goat's cheese in the middle of each one. Remove the onion halves from the ovenproof dish and place, cut side up, on top of the goat's cheese. Bring the edges of the pastry up to meet the sides of the goat's cheese and crimp all round the edge of each tart, then bake in the oven for 25 minutes.

4. Meanwhile, remove the thyme and garlic from the ovenproof dish and pour in the extra-virgin olive oil to make a dressing, seasoning with salt and pepper to taste. Place the rocket in a bowl, drizzle over 4 tablespoons of the dressing from the dish and toss together.

5. Remove the tarts from the oven, pour over any leftover dressing and serve straight away with the dressed rocket salad on the side.

FLAGEOLET BEANS, TOMATOES AND ROSEMARY ON TOAST

A kind of posh beans on toast, which kids and adults will both love. You can serve the beans as a garnish for load of other recipes, too. The flavours work with duck, beef and lamb, or with roasted fish like cod or monkfish.

SERVES 4

VEGETARIAN

50g (2oz) butter

2 shallots, peeled and diced

4 cloves of garlic, peeled and finely chopped

75ml (3fl oz) white wine

1 x 400g can of chopped tomatoes

4 tomatoes, roughly chopped

1 x 400g can of flageolet beans, drained and rinsed

Leaves from 2 sprigs of rosemary, finely chopped

25g (1oz) flat-leaf parsley, chopped

4 thick slices of white or brown bread

30ml (1¼fl oz) extra-virgin olive oil

Salt and black pepper

1. Melt a third of the butter in a large casserole dish over a medium heat, add the shallots and garlic and sauté, without browning, for 3–4 minutes. Add the wine, canned and fresh tomatoes and beans to the pan, along with 100ml (3½fl oz) of water.

2. Bring to the boil, then reduce the heat, add the rosemary and simmer for 15 minutes to thicken the mixture and break down the fresh tomatoes. To finish, add the parsley and remaining butter and season with salt and pepper.

3. Just before the bean mixture has finished cooking, toast the bread on both sides, placing a slice on each plate. Top with the beans and a good drizzle of olive oil and serve immediately.

DOUBLE-BAKED EMMENTAL SOUFFLÉS WITH KIRSCH

A good dinner-party dish that can be made in advance, as it's the second stage of cooking that causes the soufflés to rise. Put plenty of sauce and cheese on the top when cooking for the second time, to stop the soufflé drying out and to colour the finished dish. Try mixing the cheeses if you want a different flavour, though I would steer away from blue cheese as it overpowers the whole thing.

SERVES 6
VEGETARIAN

50g (2oz) butter, plus extra for greasing
50g (2oz) plain flour
300ml (11fl oz) milk
¼ tsp freshly grated nutmeg
150g (5oz) Emmental cheese, grated, plus extra to serve
Grated zest of 1 lemon
5 egg yolks
500ml (18fl oz) egg whites
Salt and black pepper

FOR THE SAUCE
2 litres (3½ pints) double cream
Juice of 1 lemon
250ml (9fl oz) kirsch
200g (7oz) Emmental cheese, grated

SIX 6–7.5CM (2½–3IN) DIAMETER RAMEKINS

1. Preheat the oven to 180°C (350°F), Gas 4, and grease the ramekins.

2. Melt the butter in a large, non-stick saucepan over a low heat, stir in the flour and heat for 2 minutes to cook the flour, then gradually add the milk, mixing well between each addition. Add the nutmeg, stir in the cheese and lemon zest and remove the pan from the heat. Allow to cool, then season with salt and pepper and fold in the egg yolks.

3. Whisk the egg whites into soft peaks and fold into the mixture, then divide between the greased ramekins and bake in the oven for 12–15 minutes.

4. Remove from the oven and allow to cool, then carefully remove from the ramekins. (The soufflés can now be finished immediately or kept in the fridge for up to 24 hours.)

5. When you are ready to serve, preheat the oven to 200°C (400°F), Gas 6. Remove the soufflés from the fridge and place in an ovenproof dish. Combine all the ingredients for the sauce and pour over the soufflés. Scatter over some extra cheese, then reheat in the oven for 8–10 minutes or until golden brown.

CHAPTER 8
SALADS

DRESSING A SALAD

The basic ingredients of a salad dressing are an oil – made either from pressed olives or some type of vegetable, nut or seed – and an acid, whether lemon juice or vinegar or a combination of them both. If vinegar is used, then the dressing is referred to as a vinaigrette. A basic dressing would be just olive oil with lemon juice or vinegar – usually 4 parts oil to 1 part lemon juice/vinegar. A light sherry vinaigrette (see page 152) is also very simple – it's the one we use as our house dressing as the flavour complements most mixed leaves without overpowering them. It also goes well with other raw vegetables, such as peppers, tomatoes or radishes. The lemon vinaigrette works well with crisp lettuce leaves like cos or Little Gem, especially when accompanying fish, but don't dress the salad too early or the acid in the dressing will break down the leaves and make them wilt.

The biggest dilemma when dressing a salad is whether to season the dressing or the salad. As you'll see, some of the dressings here include salt and pepper while others don't. For lighter dressings, used with lighter-flavoured leaves, I season the salad *not* the dressing. For stronger-flavoured dressings, such as the one made with roast garlic (see page 153), it is better to season the dressing rather than the salad.

HERB VINAIGRETTE

MAKES ABOUT 175ML (6FL OZ)
VEGETARIAN

2 tsp Dijon mustard
25ml (1fl oz) white wine vinegar
25ml (1fl oz) champagne vinegar
125ml (4½fl oz) olive oil
1 shallot, peeled and finely chopped
1 tbsp chopped flat-leaf parsley
1 tbsp chopped chives
2 tbsp chopped chervil
1 tbsp chopped tarragon

To make the dressing, first place the mustard in a bowl. Gradually whisk in the white wine and champagne vinegars, then add the olive oil in a thin stream, whisking constantly until the dressing is emulsified and smooth. Add the shallot, then just before serving add the chopped herbs and mix well. This dressing can be kept in the fridge, in a covered container, for up to a week.

SHERRY VINAIGRETTE

MAKES 400ML (14FL OZ)
VEGETARIAN

50ml (2fl oz) sherry vinegar
50ml (2fl oz) red wine vinegar
300ml (11fl oz) extra-virgin olive oil

Place the sherry and red wine vinegars in a bowl and whisk in three-quarters of the olive oil. Check the flavour for the balance of oil and acidity, adding more oil if needed. This dressing, if placed in a clean bottle or jar with a screw-top lid, will keep for up to a month.

LEMON VINAIGRETTE

MAKES 400ML (14FL OZ)
VEGETARIAN

75ml (3fl oz) white wine vinegar
Juice of 3 lemons
175ml (6fl oz) extra-virgin olive oil
1 shallot, peeled and finely chopped
2 tsp chopped chives

Whisk the vinegar and lemon juice together in a bowl, then pour in the olive oil in a steady stream, whisking well until the dressing is emulsified and smooth. Add the chopped shallot and chives and use the dressing within a day – the acidity of the lemon juice will cause the chives to go brown otherwise.

BUTTERMILK DRESSING

MAKES 300ML (11FL OZ)
VEGETARIAN

125ml (4½fl oz) mayonnaise

50ml (2fl oz) buttermilk

75ml (3fl oz) double cream

Juice of 1 lemon

5 tbsp chopped herbs, such as parsley, chives and dill

1 shallot, peeled and finely chopped

Salt and white pepper

Place the mayonnaise in a bowl, then add the remaining ingredients and whisk together until combined but being careful not to over-whip. Season to taste with salt and pepper.

ROAST GARLIC DRESSING

MAKES 225ML (8FL OZ)
VEGETARIAN

1 bulb of garlic, smoked or unsmoked

175ml (6fl oz) extra-virgin olive oil

50ml (2fl oz) white wine vinegar

Salt and black pepper

1. Preheat the oven to 200°C (400°F), Gas 6.

2. Cut the garlic bulb in half crossways and place one of the halves in an ovenproof dish, reserving the remaining half to use in other recipes. Drizzle with some of the olive oil, cover with foil and roast in the oven for 30 minutes, then remove and allow to cool.

3. Squeeze the garlic out of the cloves, place in a blender with the vinegar and whizz to a paste. Pour in the olive oil while blending, then transfer to a bowl, adding salt and pepper to taste. Use straight away or cover and keep in the fridge for up to 2 weeks.

MUSTARD VINAIGRETTE

MAKES 375ML (13FL OZ)
VEGETARIAN

2 tsp Dijon mustard

75ml (3fl oz) white wine vinegar

300ml (11fl oz) extra-virgin olive oil

1 tsp wholegrain mustard

Place the Dijon mustard in a bowl with the vinegar and slowly pour in the olive oil in a thin stream, whisking constantly until the dressing is emulsified and smooth. Whisk in the wholegrain mustard, cover the bowl and refrigerate. This will keep for up to 2 weeks in the fridge.

JODY'S MOZZARELLA WITH PAN-FRIED FIGS AND MINT

Ex-Formula One racing driver Jody Scheckter recently bought a farm in Hampshire. Now he is responsible for some of the best produce in my area, including lamb, beef and pork, and even beer. He has begun producing mozzarella and it's as good, if not better, than the Italian variety. It should be eaten as fresh as possible because the salt water it's stored in tends to break down the cheese if left for any length of time.

SERVES 4

VEGETARIAN

2 x 200g balls of mozzarella cheese

75ml (3fl oz) extra-virgin olive oil, plus 1 tbsp for frying

8 large fresh black figs

12 mint leaves, stalks removed

50ml (2fl oz) balsamic vinegar

Sea salt and black pepper

1. Drain the mozzarella balls and cut each into 8 wedges.

2. Place a large, non-stick frying pan over a medium heat and pour in 1 tablespoon of the olive oil, then cut the figs in half and season with salt and pepper. Lay the figs in the pan cut side down and cook for 2 minutes, then turn over and cook for a further minute. Remove from the heat and set aside.

3. Rip up the mint leaves and sprinkle over the figs, then transfer the figs from the pan to the plates and add the mozzarella pieces.

4. Return the pan to the heat, pour in the balsamic vinegar and bring to the boil, then remove from the heat and whisk in the remaining olive oil. Season with salt and pepper, then spoon the dressing over the figs and mozzarella and serve.

GRILLED PEAR AND GORGONZOLA SALAD WITH ROASTED HAZELNUTS

If you're short on time, you can make this with good-quality canned pears: drain and dry well, brush lightly with oil, then chargrill to get a better flavour. Most types of blue cheese work with pears, so it's up to you which one you use.

SERVES 4
VEGETARIAN

75g (3oz) hazelnuts
2 ripe pears
2–3 tbsp olive oil
50g (2oz) watercress
50g (2oz) frisée lettuce leaves
150g (5oz) Gorgonzola cheese, diced
Salt and black pepper

FOR THE DRESSING
3 tbsp white wine vinegar
1 tbsp caster sugar
1 tbsp chopped chives
150ml (5fl oz) extra-virgin olive oil

1. First roast and peel the hazelnuts. Preheat the oven to 200°C (400°F), Gas 6. Place the hazelnuts on a baking tray and roast for 15–20 minutes or until the skins split. Remove from the oven, tip into a clean tea towel and rub to remove the skins, then allow to cool and roughly crush with a rolling pin.

2. Set a griddle pan or a large, non-stick frying pan over a high heat. Peel the pears, remove the core and slice each lengthways into 6 pieces, then drizzle with the olive oil and season with salt and pepper.

3. Mix the salad leaves together in a large bowl, then divide between plates for serving. Place the pears in the heated pan and briefly cook on all sides, allowing them to get chargrill marks if using the griddle pan, then remove from the heat and set aside.

4. To make the dressing, place the vinegar, sugar and chives in a bowl and gradually whisk in the olive oil.

5. Place the pears on the salad leaves, allowing 3 slices per portion, crumble the cheese over the top, followed by the hazelnuts, then spoon over the dressing and serve.

WARM SALAD OF DUCK EGG, CROÛTONS AND PECORINO

I'm really glad that duck eggs are now available in supermarkets. The colour and richness of the yolks makes them ideal for dishes like this and they make great scrambled eggs. They can also be used in baking as a substitute for hen's eggs. Pecorino is a hard sheep's-milk cheese, saltier than Parmesan but with the same texture. In Italy I've been served this famous cheese at the end of the meal simply drizzled with chestnut honey.

SERVES 4
VEGETARIAN

6 medium-sized duck eggs

100g (3½oz) asparagus spears, woody ends snapped off

3–4 tbsp olive oil

2 slices of white bread, crusts removed and cut into croûtons

Leaves from 2 dandelion plants

50g (2oz) watercress

Juice of 2 lemons

6 tbsp extra-virgin olive oil

150g (5oz) pecorino, shaved with a potato peeler

Sea salt and black pepper

1. Place a saucepan of water on the hob and bring to the boil, season with salt, add the duck eggs and boil for 4 minutes, then remove from the pan and into cold water. Allow the eggs to cool before peeling off the shells.

2. Place a griddle pan or frying pan over a high heat, brush the asparagus spears with half the olive oil, season with salt and pepper and fry in the pan for 4–5 minutes or until tender, allowing them to get chargrill marks if using a griddle pan.

3. In another frying pan, quickly sauté the croûtons in the remaining oil for 2–3 minutes or until browned, then transfer on to kitchen paper to drain.

4. Mix the salad leaves together in a bowl, then combine the lemon juice and extra-virgin olive oil in another bowl and season with salt and pepper. Divide the salad leaves between plates, then cut the eggs in half and place 3 halves in the centre of each plate. Scatter the asparagus, croûtons and pecorino shavings over the salad, spoon over the dressing and serve.

ASPARAGUS, FETA AND SPINACH WITH HONEY AND POPPY SEED DRESSING

English asparagus has a really short season, lasting just some eight weeks, which is a shame because it tastes so good. You can chargrill or barbecue it from raw, though I like to blanch mine first, as I think it improves the taste.

SERVES 4
VEGETARIAN

24 asparagus spears, blanched (see method on page 48) and cooled

2–3 tbsp olive oil

100g (3½oz) baby spinach

100g (3½oz) watercress

200g (7oz) feta cheese, diced

Salt and black pepper

FOR THE DRESSING

2 tbsp runny honey

2 tsp white wine vinegar

2 tsp blue poppy seeds

150ml (5fl oz) rapeseed oil

1. Place a griddle pan or non-stick frying pan over a high heat, drizzle the asparagus spears with the olive oil, season with salt and pepper and fry for 2–3 minutes, turning them over continuously to allow the spears to brown – and get chargrill marks if using the griddle pan – then set aside.

2. Mix the spinach and watercress leaves together in a bowl and season with salt and pepper. To make the dressing, put the honey in another bowl, along with the white wine vinegar and poppy seeds, and whisk in the rapeseed oil.

3. Lay 6 asparagus spears on each plate, arrange the mixed leaves on the side, crumbling the feta cheese over the top, then spoon over the dressing and serve with crusty bread.

CHICKEN CAESAR SALAD WITH ROSEMARY CROÛTONS

A good trick with this classic salad is to cook the garlic before making the dressing. Doing so will bring out the flavour of the garlic but without any unpleasant aftertaste. Once made, the dressing will keep in the fridge for 3–4 days.

SERVES 4

150ml (5fl oz) white wine

4 cloves of garlic, peeled

25g (1oz) butter

2 thick slices of white bloomer (crusts removed), cut into cubes

1 tsp chopped rosemary leaves

4 egg yolks, beaten

2 canned anchovy fillets

150g (5oz) Parmesan cheese, freshly grated, plus extra to serve

300ml (11fl oz) vegetable oil

1 tbsp Dijon mustard

Leaves from 1 cos lettuce

2 cooked chicken breasts, sliced

Salt and black pepper

1. Pour the wine into a saucepan, add the garlic and boil for about 5 minutes or until the cloves are soft. Remove from the heat and set aside to cool.

2. Melt the butter in a frying pan over a medium heat, add the bread cubes and the rosemary and sauté for 2–3 minutes or until golden brown.

3. Pour the wine and garlic into a bowl, add the egg yolks, anchovy fillets and cheese and blend using a hand-held blender, adding the vegetable oil in a steady stream. (It's best to add the oil slowly to stop the mixture from splitting, although the cheese in the dressing should help blend everything together.) Add the mustard and season to taste with salt and pepper.

4. Place the lettuce leaves and chicken in a serving bowl, then add the croûtons and pour over the dressing. Toss together well, season with salt and pepper and divide between plates, topping with more freshly grated Parmesan to serve.

WATERMELON, FETA AND ORANGE SALAD WITH BASIL

This salad is a bit of a curved ball in this book, as it's not the type of food I normally cook. However, it's one of the dishes from my travels that I just can't get out of my head. Fresh and colourful, it does really need to be eaten in sunny weather though, I think.

SERVES 4

VEGETARIAN

200g (7oz) watermelon flesh, deseeded and cut into 1cm (½in) dice

175g (6oz) feta cheese, cut into 5mm (¼in) strips or 1cm (½in) dice

Peeled segments and leftover juice of 2 oranges

Inner leaves of 2 Little Gem lettuces

10 fresh basil leaves

8 tbsp extra-virgin olive oil

Salt and black pepper

1. Place the watermelon in a large bowl, along with the feta, orange segments and lettuce leaves, and toss together very gently. Tear up the basil leaves and add them to the salad.

2. Add enough olive oil to coat the ingredients, season with salt and pepper and gently mix again, then arrange on individual plates, spoon over the orange juice and serve.

'Trust your palate, the best dishes come when you cook to what you like, not what you think they will like.'
NIC WATT

GOAT'S CHEESE, BEETROOT AND HAZELNUT SALAD

This is a dish we serve in the restaurant. We make it with smoked beetroot, which is a bit fiddly, so this is a simpler version. Beetroot is a vegetable I have been using more and more over the years. I love it either in salads or simply roasted.

SERVES 4
VEGETARIAN

4 thick slices of white bread, crusts removed

200g (7oz) goat's cheese, sliced into 4

300g (11oz) cooked beetroot (not in vinegar), peeled and sliced

100g (3½oz) rocket

3 tbsp chopped chervil, to garnish

FOR THE DRESSING

25ml (1fl oz) white wine vinegar

2 tsp Dijon mustard

Pinch of caster sugar

100ml (3½fl oz) olive oil

50g (2oz) hazelnuts, roasted and peeled (see page 156), then roughly chopped

Salt and black pepper

1. To make the dressing, place the white wine vinegar, Dijon mustard and sugar in a bowl and whisk until combined, then slowly whisk in the olive oil, add the chopped nuts, season with salt and pepper and set aside.

2. Preheat the grill to high.

3. Cut each slice of bread to fit the goat's cheese and toast on both sides under the grill, then put a slice of cheese on each piece of toast and place back under the grill, toasting for 2–3 minutes or until golden brown on top.

4. Arrange the sliced beetroot in the centre of each plate, place some of the rocket leaves on top with a goat's cheese croûton on top of that, drizzle some of the dressing over and around, sprinkle with the chervil and serve.

PUY LENTIL SALAD WITH RED WINE VINEGAR AND GRILLED GOAT'S CHEESE

This may look like it needs a lot of ingredients and, to be honest, it does, but it's really worth it. I first came across cooked lentils while working in France, they are great and not just for people who wear sandals. They are nice cold in salads but need an acid such as lemon, lime or vinegar. (Though don't use malt vinegar – that's for your chips! Instead, use balsamic or sherry vinegar.)

SERVES 4
VEGETARIAN

25g (1oz) butter

½ leek, trimmed and finely chopped

1 shallot, peeled and finely chopped

½ carrot, peeled and finely chopped

1 clove of garlic, peeled and finely chopped

100g (3½oz) Puy lentils

100ml (3½fl oz) red wine

400ml (14fl oz) vegetable stock or water

3 tbsp balsamic vinegar

1 bay leaf

4 slices of baguette

200ml (7fl oz) extra-virgin olive oil

4 x 50g (2oz) goat's cheeses

1 tbsp chopped chives

1 tbsp chopped chervil

1 tbsp chopped flat-leaf parsley

4 tbsp red wine vinegar

Salt and black pepper

1. Melt the butter in a large, heavy-based saucepan over a medium heat and when it begins to bubble, add the chopped leek, shallot, carrot and garlic, and sauté, without browning, for 2 minutes.

2. Add the lentils, red wine, stock or water, balsamic vinegar and bay leaf and bring to the boil, then reduce the heat and simmer for about 25 minutes or until the lentils are tender. Remove from the heat and pour into a bowl, draining off any excess liquid.

3. While the lentils are cooking, preheat the grill to high.

4. Place the bread slices in the grill pan, drizzle with 50ml (2fl oz) of the olive oil and season with salt and pepper, then toast under the grill until golden brown on both sides. Remove from the grill, top with the goat's cheeses, drizzle with 25ml (1fl oz) of the oil and place back under the grill for 2 minutes to brown on top.

5. To finish the lentil salad, add all the chopped herbs, then the red wine vinegar and the remaining olive oil and season to taste with salt and pepper. Spoon on to plates, top with the goat's cheese croûtons and serve.

SCALLOPS WITH BABY COS, APPLES AND CASHEW NUTS

Hand-dived scallops are obviously the ideal option for this recipe, but you can also get hold of pre-packaged scallops, which are good if you're short on time or nervous about removing them from the shells. Putting vanilla with fish isn't a new combination – the French have been doing it for a long time and it really works, granted not with all fish, but with most white flesh types.

SERVES 4

White meat from 20 hand-dived scallops (see method for opening scallops on page 29)

50g (2oz) unsalted butter, softened

1 vanilla pod, seeds scraped out and retained

2 baby cos lettuces or inner leaves of 1 standard cos lettuce

2 Golden Delicious apples, unpeeled

Juice of 1 lemon

1–2 tbsp olive oil

100g (3½oz) cashew nuts

2 tsp chopped chives

Salt and black pepper

1. Rinse the scallop meat and pat dry on kitchen paper, then transfer to a plate and place in the fridge.

2. Place the butter in a bowl and whisk in the vanilla seeds until combined, then set aside.

3. Place the lettuce leaves in another bowl, slice the apples, discarding the core, then cut into matchstick-sized pieces, drizzle with a little of the lemon juice and add to the bowl with the lettuce.

4. Place a non-stick frying pan over a medium heat, drizzle with the olive oil and add the scallops. Fry for 1 minute or until browned, then season with salt and pepper, turn the scallops over and cook for 30 seconds on the other side. Tip in the cashew nuts, tossing them with the scallops, then add the vanilla butter to the pan and remove from the heat. Sprinkle over the chives and allow to rest for 1 minute.

5. Arrange the salad leaves and apple pieces on the plates, spoon over the nuts and then the scallops. Pour over the melted butter and serve.

CHAPTER 9
SIDES

BASIC WHITE SAUCE

White sauce is the basis for so much in cooking, from a simple cheese sauce to more advanced dishes like soufflé. The problem I've found with many white sauce recipes is that there is too much flour added right at the start, which gives the sauce an odd taste and makes the consistency too thick. The basic rule is to make sure the flour is added only once the butter has melted and to then cook it for a minute or two before adding liquid.

1. First melt the butter in a heavy-based saucepan over a medium heat.

2. Once melted add the flour, remove from the heat and stir in well.

3. This mixture of flour and melted butter is called a roux.

MAKES 450ML (16FL OZ)

* *25g (1oz) butter*
* *25g (1oz) plain flour*
* *400ml (14fl oz) milk*

4. Place back over the heat and mix for 2 minutes.

5. Reduce the heat and slowly add the milk, while mixing or whisking all the time, until all the milk has been incorporated.

6. Increase the heat and simmer for 5 minutes, stirring all the time with a wooden spoon, then remove and use as required.

CHORIZO AND CHILLI ROAST POTATOES

Chorizo goes brilliantly with potato because it has such a strong taste and a totally contrasting texture. This dish makes a great tapas-like snack or is nice served with a pan-fried cod fillet.

SERVES 4

500g (1lb 2oz) all-round potatoes, such as Vivaldi, unpeeled

300g (11oz) chorizo sausage, skin removed

1 red chilli, deseeded and diced

150ml (5fl oz) olive oil

4 tsp chopped flat-leaf parsley

Salt and black pepper

1. Preheat the oven to 200°C (400°F), Gas 6.

2. Chop the potatoes and the chorizo into 2.5cm (1in) dice, then place the diced potatoes in a roasting tin and season with salt and pepper. Sprinkle over the chilli and the diced chorizo, pour over the olive oil and bake in the oven for 45 minutes, occasionally turning them over so that they are evenly browned.

3. When the potatoes are cooked, remove from the oven and mix in the chopped parsley. Tip into a warmed dish and serve immediately.

CAULIFLOWER CHEESE

If you follow the advice and pictures for the white sauce on pages 166–7, then you can't go wrong with this dish. Once you've made it, cover it up until you're ready to serve, otherwise it will form a skin on top, which ends up making it lumpy. Feel free to mix and match the types of cheese you use.

SERVES 4
VEGETARIAN

1 large cauliflower, cut into small florets

50g (2oz) mature Cheddar cheese, grated

Salt and black pepper

FOR THE SAUCE
1 clove

1 bay leaf

1 small onion, peeled

600ml (1 pint) milk

25g (1oz) butter

25g (1oz) plain flour

1 tsp English mustard

Pinch of freshly grated nutmeg

200ml (7fl oz) double cream

200g (7oz) mature Cheddar cheese, grated

ONE 20–25CM (8–10IN) SQUARE OVENPROOF DISH

1. To make the sauce, first stud the clove through the bay leaf and into the onion and place in a saucepan with the milk. Gently warm over a low heat, allowing the milk to be infused with the flavour of the onion and spices.

2. Make a roux by melting the butter in a heavy-based saucepan. Once melted, add the flour and cook over a low heat for 2–3 minutes, stirring all the time and making sure the roux doesn't stick to the bottom of the pan. Pour in the infused milk (having removed the studded onion), a little at a time, stirring constantly until all the milk has been incorporated, then gently simmer for 5–6 minutes over a low heat.

3. Stir in the mustard, nutmeg, cream and Cheddar, allowing the cheese to melt, then remove from the heat, season with salt and pepper and set aside.

4. Meanwhile, preheat the oven to 200°C (400°F), Gas 6.

5. Bring a large saucepan of salted water to the boil, drop in the cauliflower florets and bring back up to the boil. Cook for 1–2 minutes or until just tender, then remove and plunge into cold water to cool. Place in a colander and set aside to drain.

6. Pour a little of the cheese sauce into the ovenproof dish, scatter the cauliflower florets over the top, then pour the remainder of the sauce over the cauliflower. Sprinkle over the grated cheese and bake in the oven for 30 minutes or until golden brown.

LEEK AND BRIOCHE GRATIN

This gratin is delicious and goes well with roast chicken or beef. Brioche is much better to use in it than white breadcrumbs because it has a nicer flavour and helps to stop the gratin from drying out in the oven.

SERVES 8
VEGETARIAN

250g (9oz) brioche (crusts removed), cut into 2.5cm (1in) dice

50ml (2fl oz) extra-virgin olive oil

4 sprigs of thyme

50g (2oz) unsalted butter

2 leeks, trimmed and cut into 1cm (½in) slices

1 white onion, peeled and roughly chopped

250g (9oz) Comté cheese, grated

3 eggs

200ml (7fl oz) milk

200ml (7fl oz) double cream

1 bay leaf

Salt and black pepper

ONE 23 X 33CM (9 X 13IN) OVENPROOF DISH

1. Preheat the oven to 200°C (400°F), Gas 6.

2. Place the diced brioche on a baking tray, drizzle with the olive oil and add the thyme, then bake in the oven for 8–10 minutes to lightly brown.

3. Meanwhile, melt the butter in a large saucepan over a medium heat, add the leeks and onion and cook for 8–10 minutes to soften but without browning.

4. While the brioche and leeks are both cooking, sprinkle one-third of the cheese into the ovenproof dish. Break the eggs into a separate bowl, pour in the milk and cream and whisk together, seasoning well with salt and pepper.

5. Scatter the toasted brioche pieces in the ovenproof dish and spoon over the cooked leeks. Pour over the cream mixture and add the bay leaf, then sprinkle with the remaining cheese and bake in the oven for 25 minutes or until set and golden brown on top.

BRAISED RED CABBAGE WITH ROASTED HAZELNUTS AND PANCETTA

I love red cabbage, but it does need to be cooked for long enough, not only to make it taste better, but also to soften the cabbage so that it's not crunchy. The colour of this dish always adds some interest to your plate no matter what you serve it with. For the Parsnip and Potato Mash in the photograph, see page 184.

SERVES 4

75ml (3fl oz) olive oil

2 onions, peeled and sliced

½ red cabbage, core removed and leaves thinly sliced

100g (3½oz) demerara or soft dark brown sugar

250ml (9fl oz) red wine

3 tbsp redcurrant jelly

200g (7oz) pancetta, diced

100g (3½oz) hazelnuts, roasted, peeled and chopped (see method on page 156)

2 tbsp chopped flat-leaf parsley

Salt and black pepper

1. Place a heavy-based saucepan over a medium heat, pour in 50ml (2fl oz) of the olive oil, add the onions and sauté, without browning, for 2–3 minutes. Tip in the cabbage and cook for 2–3 minutes, then mix in the sugar. Add the red wine and redcurrant jelly and bring to the boil, then reduce the heat, cover with a lid and simmer gently for 20 minutes.

2. Meanwhile, in a non-stick frying pan, sauté the pancetta in the remaining olive oil over a high heat for 2–3 minutes or until golden brown, then drain on kitchen paper and set aside.

3. After 20 minutes, remove the lid from the saucepan and continue cooking to allow some of the liquid to evaporate. Add the hazelnuts and the pancetta, mixing them in well. Season slightly, sprinkle over the parsley, then remove from the heat and serve.

VICHY CARROTS

This method of cooking vegetables comes from the town of Vichy in France, famous for its spring water. The cooked veg has a really delicious flavour, partly because all the flavour is kept in the pan and also because, as the water reduces, the butter and sugar emulsify to make a sauce. Carrots are the best to cook like this, and at Christmas you can do your parsnips this way, with a touch of sherry to add to the taste.

SERVES 4
VEGETARIAN

25g (1oz) butter
1 tbsp caster sugar
Splash of boiling water
400g (14oz) Chantenay carrots

Place a small saucepan over a medium heat and add the butter, sugar and water. Once the butter has melted, add the carrots and place a lid on the pan, then cook for 6–8 minutes or until tender.

WILTED CHARD WITH HAZELNUTS

Chard is a vegetable that has been going nuts in my garden and therefore I've been using it quite a lot lately. It works well with all types of nuts, but I like it best with hazelnuts.

SERVES 4
VEGETARIAN

75g (3oz) unsalted butter
400g (14oz) chard leaves, stalks removed
25g (1oz) hazelnuts, roasted and peeled (see page 156) then lightly chopped
Salt and black pepper

Place a large, heavy-based saucepan over a medium heat and add the butter. Allow it to melt slightly then add the chard, cover with a lid, reduce the heat and gently sweat for 2–3 minutes. Remove the lid and cook for a further minute or two to allow the moisture to evaporate, then mix in the hazelnuts and season with salt and pepper. Drain to get rid of any remaining liquid, then place in a warmed serving dish.

MINTED PEAS

Peas are one of the joys of growing your own – that's if they aren't all eaten straight out of the pod while you're still stood in the vegetable patch! This is a simple, classic dish, but one that will always be a favourite.

SERVES 4
VEGETARIAN

500g (1lb 2oz) peas
(fresh or frozen)

50g (2oz) mint leaves, chopped

50g (2oz) unsalted butter

Salt

Bring a saucepan of salted water to the boil, plunge the peas in and cook for 2–3 minutes, then drain. Add the mint leaves and butter, toss together and place in a serving dish.

CREAMED SPINACH

This quick side dish makes spinach much more interesting than just a pile of wilted leaves. It goes with most things, but it must be cooked quickly otherwise the spinach turns brown. It does need a decent amount of seasoning.

SERVES 4
VEGETARIAN

25g (1oz) unsalted butter

1 shallot, peeled and finely diced

500g (1lb 2oz) spinach, any tough
stalks removed

100g (3½oz) Comté or Emmental
cheese, grated

50ml (2fl oz) double cream

Salt and black pepper

1. Place a large, heavy-based saucepan over a medium heat and add the butter, shallot and spinach. Cover with a lid and sweat for 2–3 minutes or until the spinach is wilted, then remove the lid, stir together and drain in a sieve to get rid of any excess liquid.

2. Place in a blender with the cheese and double cream, and blitz to a purée. Alternatively, purée all the ingredients using a hand-held blender. Season well with salt and pepper and serve.

WHOLE ROASTED SHALLOTS
AND SHALLOT PURÉE

Shallots are one of my favourite vegetables and I use them a lot in my cooking, served with meat or fish. Shallot purée tastes great with fish and can be made and then kept in the fridge for a couple of days.

SERVES 4–6
VEGETARIAN

750g (1lb 10oz) shallots

100g (3½oz) caster sugar

150ml (5fl oz) double cream
(for the shallot purée)

Salt and black pepper

1. Preheat the oven to 180°C (350°F), Gas 4.

2. Peel the shallots, first blanching them in boiling water for 30 seconds, if you like, to make them easier to peel.

3. Place a large, non-stick ovenproof pan over a medium heat over a high heat, allowing it to get very hot. Toss the shallots in the sugar and drop them into the pan, then caramelise for 2–3 minutes, stirring from time to time.

4. Remove from the hob and bake in the oven for 4–5 minutes or until tender, then remove from the oven and place in a serving dish.

5. If you are making shallot purée, place the pan back over the heat, pour in the cream and bring to the boil. Remove from the heat, transfer to a blender and pulse until you have a smooth paste. Season to taste with salt and pepper and then serve.

'I've found that onions make me cry ... I'm still searching for some vegetable that makes me laugh!'
ALAIN ROUX

MUSHY PEAS WITH VINEGAR

You can alter this side dish with the addition of fresh mint but I think it's better kept nice and simple. The bicarbonate of soda is added for a few reasons: it helps to break down the peas, it retains the colour and it is also thought to prevent windy pops. Sarson's is my preferred type of vinegar.

SERVES 4
VEGETARIAN

225g (8oz) dried marrowfat peas
1 tsp bicarbonate of soda
30g (1¼oz) butter
Salt and black pepper
Malt vinegar, to serve

1. Place the peas in a large bowl and cover with 3 times their volume in cold water, add the bicarbonate of soda and allow to soak for at least 4 hours or preferably overnight.

2. Tip the peas into a colander to drain, then rinse with cold running water. Place in a large, heavy-based saucepan and cover with fresh water. Bring to the boil, then reduce the heat, cover with a lid and simmer for 1½–2 hours, stirring occasionally and adding more water if necessary to prevent the peas from drying out.

3. When cooked, the peas should have reduced to a soft mush. If they are still a bit runny, remove the lid from the pan and continue cooking for a few minutes longer to allow the liquid to evaporate. Stir in the butter and season with salt and pepper, then serve with the malt vinegar.

CREAMY POTATO MASH

For really good mash, invest in a proper potato ricer. Available online, they are a must if you want to make a light, non-lumpy mash. As, too, are butter and cream, which make it smooth and delicious.

SERVES 4–6
VEGETARIAN

900g (2lb) large floury potatoes, such as Maris Piper, peeled and quartered

150g (5oz) unsalted butter

150ml (5fl oz) double cream

Salt and white pepper

1. Place the potatoes in a large saucepan, cover with cold water and add a good pinch of salt. Bring to the boil, reduce the heat and simmer for 20–25 minutes.

2. Drain and return to the pan, placing over the heat for 1 minute to drive off any excess moisture, then remove from the heat and mash well using a potato ricer or masher.

3. Melt the butter in a separate saucepan, then pour in the cream. Bring to the boil, then remove from the heat and pour over the mashed potatoes, mixing to a smooth consistency. Season with salt and pepper as you mix, then place in a warmed dish and serve straight away.

TURNIP AND POTATO DAUPHINOIS

Dauphinois is the richest and best of all potato dishes. The trick is to be very patient, as it needs to cook in the oven for much longer than you think. Most importantly, do not add too much garlic; the dish should have just a faint whiff, not too strong a taste. The classic version is of course made just with potatoes, so if you can't get turnips then simply make the original. For a variation, you can put smoked mackerel or pancetta between the layers to add even more flavour. I love to serve dauphinois with roast lamb.

SERVES 4–6

50g (2oz) butter, softened

500g (1lb 2oz) all-round potatoes, such as Desirée

500g (1lb 2oz) turnips

300ml (11fl oz) full-fat milk

500ml (18fl oz) double cream

2 garlic cloves, peeled and finely chopped

Leaves from 2 sprigs of thyme, plus extra leaves for sprinkling

Pinch of freshly grated nutmeg

1 shallot, peeled and roughly chopped

40g (1½oz) Parmesan cheese, freshly grated

Salt and black pepper

ONE 18 X 28CM (7 X 11IN) GRATIN DISH

1. Preheat the oven to 150°C (300°F), Gas 2, and grease the gratin dish with the butter.

2. Peel the potatoes and turnips and slice as thinly as possible using a mandolin or a very sharp knife. Lay the slices on a clean tea towel and pat dry. Keep them covered with the tea towel while you prepare the rest of the ingredients.

3. Pour the milk and cream into a saucepan and add the garlic, thyme, nutmeg and shallot. Slowly heat the milk and, just as it is about to reach boiling point and you see bubbles appearing around the edges of the pan, remove it from the heat. You can strain the mixture at this point, or leave in the garlic and other flavourings for a stronger-tasting dish.

4. Layer half the potato and turnip slices in the dish, slightly overlapping the slices and sprinkling with a little salt and pepper and extra thyme leaves between each layer. You don't have to be too neat with the lower layers, but save some of your best slices for the top of the dish.

5. Pour over half the hot milk and cream, then finish off layering the rest of the potatoes and turnips. Pour over the rest of the hot milk and cream, scatter the cheese over the top and bake for about 1 hour or until golden and tender to the point of a knife.

6. Remove the dish from the oven and allow to stand for about 5 minutes to cool slightly before serving.

COLESLAW

Homemade coleslaw is so much better than the mass-produced stuff you normally find on a buffet to put with cold, bland ham! For the best result, make your own mayonnaise to use in the coleslaw, it's really worth the effort.

SERVES 4-6

400g (14oz) white cabbage, core removed and leaves finely sliced

75ml (3fl oz) white wine vinegar

1 small onion, peeled and finely sliced

2 carrots, peeled and cut into matchsticks

Dash of Tabasco sauce

Dash of Worcestershire sauce

100ml (3½fl oz) mayonnaise

100ml (3½fl oz) double cream

Sea salt and black pepper

1. Place the sliced cabbage in a large bowl and add the vinegar, then cover with cling film and allow to stand for 30 minutes.

2. Drain off the excess vinegar and add the onion and carrots, mixing them together with the cabbage. Add a dash of Tabasco and Worcestershire sauce, tossing to mix, then pour in the mayonnaise and cream. Season with salt and pepper, toss together once more and serve.

PARSNIP AND POTATO MASH

Root veg is a great way to add a twist to classic mash. You do still need to include potato, as making mash with just parsnips can be much too waxy. Try adding some sherry to give the dish a nice flavour for special occasions like Christmas dinner.

SERVES 4–6

VEGETARIAN

250g (9oz) large floury potatoes, such as Maris Piper, peeled and quartered

250g (9oz) parsnips, peeled and cut into large chunks

50g (2oz) unsalted butter

100ml (3½fl oz) milk

100ml (3½fl oz) double cream

Salt and white pepper

1. Place the potatoes in a saucepan and cover with water, add a pinch of salt and bring to the boil, then reduce the heat and simmer for 20–25 minutes or until tender. Drain and set aside.

2. Steam or boil the parsnips for 8–12 minutes, then drain and add to the pan with the potatoes. Mix them together, then mash using a masher or a potato press.

3. Place half the butter in a separate saucepan, pour in the milk and cream and bring to the boil, then remove from the heat and pour over the mashed parsnips and potatoes, mixing to a smooth consistency. Season with salt and pepper as you mix, then place in a warmed dish and serve with the remaining butter dotted on top.

CHAPTER 10
BREADS, CAKES & DESSERTS

BASIC WHITE BREAD

Making good bread isn't as easy as it may seem; it takes practice and confidence in what you're doing to get the best results. Where most people go wrong is in not making the mixture wet enough and so the finished bread ends up too doughy and dry. Once the water is added, don't go and flood the work surface with more flour as it will unbalance the recipe; instead, use olive oil if need be. The best advice I can give you is to lock the door, turn on some music and spend a day practising.

1. Sift the flour into a large bowl and add the salt, yeast, olive oil and water. (The water doesn't need to be warm: it will just take a bit longer for the dough to prove if it isn't.)

2. Mix all the ingredients into a soft dough and knead well with your hands and knuckles for about 10 minutes or until the dough is smooth and elastic in consistency.

3. Cover with a clean tea towel and leave in a warm place for 1 hour to prove.

YOU WILL NEED

* 500g (1lb 2oz) strong white flour, plus extra for dusting
* Pinch of salt
* 25g (1oz) fresh yeast or 2 x 7g sachets of fast-acting yeast
* 60ml (2½fl oz) olive oil
* 250ml (9fl oz) warm water

4. After the dough has risen and doubled in size, knock it back with your hands and tip it out on to a lightly floured work surface. Mould the dough into a rugby-ball shape, then place on a baking sheet dusted with flour and leave to rise in a warm place for a further 30 minutes.

5. Meanwhile, preheat the oven to 230°C (450°F), Gas 8. When ready to bake, dust the top of the loaf with flour and, if you like, score the top using a sharp knife.

6. Bake in the oven for 30–35 minutes. To check whether the bread is cooked, turn it over and tap the base of the loaf – it should sound hollow. Place on a wire rack to cool.

LINING A TART TIN AND BAKING BLIND

I recommend using a loose-bottomed tart tin when making a pastry case. I sometimes prefer to trim off the edges after cooking as this makes the top and edge much more uniform and prevents the sides from collapsing in on the tart. If there is masses of overhang though, do trim off the majority of it, as the raw pastry can be used for something else.

1. Grease your tart tin and lightly dust with flour. Lightly dust the work surface with flour and roll out the pastry to about 5mm (¼in) thick. To ensure a round shape to fit the tin, keep turning the pastry round as you roll it, giving a quarter turn with every 2–3 rolls. Roll out the pastry until wider all round than your tart tin.

2. Placing the rolling pin at the top of the pastry, carefully roll the pastry towards you on to the rolling pin, then, with the tart tin in front of you, unroll the pastry very gently over the tin without letting the rolling pin touch the tin.

3. Carefully push the pastry into the corners of the tin. Turn the tin with one hand and press the pastry with the other hand, making it thinner and pushing the pastry into the sides as you turn the tin.

YOU WILL NEED

* *Butter, for greasing*
* *Plain flour, for dusting*
* *1 batch of pastry (homemade or store-bought), chilled*
* *Loose-bottomed tart tin*
* *Greaseproof paper*
* *Baking beans, rice or flour*

4. Neaten the edges of the lined tart case with your rolling pin and cut away the excess pastry, then place in the fridge to rest for a minimum of 1 hour (or overnight if needed).

5. When you are ready to cook the tart case, preheat the oven to 180°C (350°F), Gas 4.

6. To line the pastry for baking 'blind', cut a sheet of greaseproof paper into a square 4–5cm (1½–2in) wider on all sides than your tin.

7. Fold the paper in half and in half again to make a smaller square, then in half diagonally to form a triangle and again to make a smaller triangle.

8. Trim the uneven edges of the folded paper triangle using your hands or a pair of scissors, and then open out the paper into a circle.

9. Place the paper circle in the tart tin, pressing it down gently.

10. Fill the lined pastry case with baking beans, uncooked rice or flour.

11. Bake, without browning, for 10 minutes, then take out of the oven and remove the beans and greaseproof paper. Place back in the oven to cook the base for 5 minutes, also without browning, then remove from the oven, carefully trim any uneven edges if needed, and fill the tart case as required.

RUM BABAS WITH CHOCOLATE SAUCE AND CHANTILLY CREAM

Britain seems to have gone baking mad recently and this retro dessert is popping up all over the place. It's just one of the delights in store for you if you've got the baking bug.

SERVES 6

VEGETARIAN

FOR THE BABAS

250g (9oz) plain flour, plus extra for dusting

Pinch of salt

15g (½oz) fresh yeast or 1 x 7g sachet of fast-acting yeast

2 eggs, beaten

15g (½oz) caster sugar

125ml (4½fl oz) milk, warmed

50g (2oz) butter, melted, plus extra for greasing

FOR THE RUM SYRUP

275g (10oz) caster sugar

125ml (4½fl oz) rum

Continued...

1. First make the babas. Sift the flour and salt into a large bowl and add the yeast. Beat the eggs with the sugar in a separate bowl, then pour in the warmed milk and stir together. Pour the egg mixture into the flour, stirring to combine, then add the melted butter and mix to make a glossy batter. Cover with a clean damp tea towel and leave in a warm place to prove for about 30 minutes or until the dough has risen and doubled in size.

2. Meanwhile, grease the savarin or dariole moulds with butter and dust with flour. When the dough has doubled in size, knock it back lightly using your hands, then divide it into 6 and transfer to the moulds. Place the filled moulds on 1–2 baking sheets and leave in a warm place to prove again for about 45 minutes.

3. While the babas are proving, preheat the oven to 200°C (400°F), Gas 6.

4. When the dough has doubled again in size, place the moulds in the oven and bake for about 10 minutes or until golden brown, then remove from the oven and turn out on to a wire rack to cool.

5. To make the rum syrup, pour 350ml (12fl oz) of water into a saucepan, add the sugar and bring to the boil. Boil for 2 minutes, then remove from the heat and allow to cool slightly. Pour 500ml (18fl oz) of the sugar syrup into a separate pan (reserving the rest of the syrup to make the chocolate sauce), add the rum and gently warm over a low heat for 1–2 minutes, then remove and allow to cool.

Continued...

RUM BABAS WITH CHOCOLATE
SAUCE AND CHANTILLY CREAM *(cont.)*

FOR THE CHOCOLATE SAUCE

75ml (3fl oz) sugar syrup (reserved when making the rum syrup)

100g (3½oz) dark chocolate (50–70% cocoa solids), broken into pieces

FOR THE CHANTILLY CREAM

300ml (11fl oz) double cream

50g (2oz) icing sugar

Few drops of vanilla extract or 1 vanilla pod

SIX 15CM (6IN) DIAMETER SAVARIN MOULDS OR 7.5CM (3IN) DARIOLE MOULDS

6. When the rum syrup has cooled, insert a fork into each baba and dunk it in the syrup, leaving it in the mixture until no more bubbles appear, then remove and place on a plate. Repeat the process with the remaining babas and set aside.

7. To make the chocolate sauce, heat the sugar syrup in a saucepan to gently warm. Remove from the heat and add the chocolate pieces, stirring until melted, then pour into a jug for serving.

8. Now make the Chantilly cream. Whip the cream in a clean bowl until soft peaks are formed, then fold in the icing sugar and vanilla extract or the seeds from the vanilla pod, and serve with the warm babas and chocolate sauce.

'A chef's day is never done. Even the beers after work are research and development.'
STUART GILLIES

SPECK SANDWICH SOLDIERS WITH SOFT-BOILED EGGS

This is a fun dish I once served as a canapé at a dinner party and it went down really well. The soldiers are a bit of work, but worth it for their deliciousness when dunked into the egg. Try adding a little mustard with the ham if you'd like more of a kick.

SERVES 4

50g (2oz) butter, softened, plus extra for greasing
8 thin slices of white bread
1 large egg white
8 thin slices of speck or Parma ham
4 large eggs
Rock salt and black pepper

1. Preheat the grill to high and the oven to 180°C (350°F), Gas 4, then grease a baking tray with butter.

2. Place the slices of bread under the grill and toast on one side only. Meanwhile, place the egg white in a bowl and whisk to a foam with a fork. Remove the bread from the grill and brush the non-toasted side of each slice with the whisked egg white. Place 2 slices of speck or Parma ham on top of half the slices of bread, then top each with a remaining slice, toasted side up.

3. Spread the tops of the toasted sandwiches with butter, top with another baking tray and press down a little before placing in the oven, with the tray still on top, and baking for 6–8 minutes.

4. Just before the sandwiches have finished cooking, place the eggs in a saucepan and cover with water. Bring to the boil, then reduce the heat and gently simmer for 2 minutes before removing from the water. Blanch in cold water for 10 seconds and then place in the egg cups and remove the tops.

5. Remove the crusts from the toasted sandwiches and cut into soldiers, then arrange these around the soft-boiled eggs and serve, seasoning with salt and pepper to individual taste.

CHOCOLATE, MINT AND SATSUMA BREAD

This is an unusual bread that combines three strong flavours and is sweet and moreish. It is a delight toasted for breakfast or eaten on its own at any time of day. Don't feel you have to make the loaves smooth or tidy – it looks great a bit rustic.

MAKES 2 SMALL LOAVES
VEGETARIAN

500g (1lb 2oz) strong white flour, plus extra for dusting

8g (⅓oz) salt

40g (1½oz) caster sugar

50g (2oz) butter, diced and softened

25g (1oz) fresh yeast or 2 x 7g sachets of fast-acting yeast

200ml (7fl oz) warm water

200g (7oz) dark chocolate chips or dark chocolate chopped into small pieces

10 mint leaves, roughly chopped

1 x 250g can of satsumas, drained

1. Sift the flour and salt into a large bowl, then add the sugar, butter and yeast. Pour in the water, a little at a time, and begin to mix by hand until you have a dough that is sticky but pliable. Try not to make the dough too stiff as this will result in a hard loaf of bread once cooked. Add a little more warm water, if needed, to ensure that the dough remains pliable.

2. Place the dough on a lightly floured work surface and knead with your hands for 7–8 minutes, then mould it into a ball and place in the bowl. Cover with a clean damp tea towel and set aside to rest somewhere warm for 1 hour or until it has risen and doubled in size.

3. Knock the dough back lightly and tip it out on to a floured work surface, then carefully mix the chocolate chips, mint leaves and satsuma pieces into the dough by hand.

4. Divide the dough into 2 equal portions, roll each piece into a sphere and flatten with your hands into the shape of a rugby ball. Place the loaves on a floured baking sheet with the folds in the dough underneath. Sprinkle with flour, then score the top with a sharp knife and place somewhere warm for another hour to double in size again.

5. Meanwhile, preheat the oven to 220°C (425°F), Gas 7.

6. Bake the loaves in the oven for 25 minutes. They are cooked when the base of each loaf sounds hollow when you tap it. Remove from the oven and place on a wire rack to cool.

GRISSINI STICKS WITH PARMA HAM

I started making these grissini sticks only recently, after a trip to an Italian bakery. And the idea of wrapping them in ham was inspired by a trip to the stunning Venice Cipriani hotel: when you get off the boat, they put one of these sticks in one of your hands and a glass of bubbles in the other. I think I ate ten of these little things, at least!

SERVES 4

16 grissini sticks (either homemade as below or bought)

16 thin slices of Parma ham

Extra-virgin olive oil, for drizzling

Cracked black pepper

FOR THE GRISSINI (OPTIONAL) (MAKES 20–24 STICKS)

50g (2oz) unsalted butter, plus extra for greasing

175ml (6fl oz) milk

1 x 7g sachet of fast-acting yeast

350g (12oz) plain flour, plus extra for dusting

½ tsp fine salt

1. If you are making the grissini sticks yourself, place the butter and milk in a saucepan over a low heat and gently warm, then remove from the heat and whisk in the yeast.

2. Sift the flour and salt into a large bowl and gradually mix in the warmed milk, a little at a time. When all the milk has been incorporated and you have a soft dough (add a little more warm milk if it seems too dry), turn it out on to a lightly floured work surface and gently knead for 2 minutes, then place on a baking tray lightly greased with butter. Cover with a clean damp tea towel and leave in the fridge to rest for 25 minutes.

3. Remove from the fridge and fold the dough over to form a square, then cover with the cloth and allow to rest again in the fridge for a further 25 minutes. Meanwhile, preheat the oven to 200°C (400°F), Gas 6, and lightly grease a baking sheet with butter.

4. Remove the dough from the tray and place on a work surface very lightly dusted with flour. Using a sharp knife, cut off a thin slice about 10cm (4in) long, then roll this into a stick shape and place on the baking sheet. Repeat this process with the remainder of the dough, then bake in the oven for 10–12 minutes without browning (or until very lightly coloured). Remove from the oven and place on a wire rack to cool.

5. To serve, lay a slice of Parma ham on a chopping board, place a grissini stick at one end and roll it up in the ham. Repeat this process with 15 other sticks, drizzle with a little olive oil and sprinkle with the pepper, then arrange in a tall glass.

TOASTED BANANA BREAD WITH CARAMELISED BANANAS

This is my type of dish, and the flavour of the banana bread gets even better if you make it in advance. It can be eaten as cake any time you want, but it's most delicious served as a dessert with the bananas and ice cream.

SERVES 4

VEGETARIAN

100g (3½oz) unsalted butter, plus extra for greasing

200g (7oz) plain flour, plus extra for dusting

100g (3½oz) caster sugar

2 over-ripe bananas

2 eggs, beaten

1 tsp baking powder

50ml (2fl oz) milk (optional)

Whipped cream, to serve

FOR THE CARAMELISED BANANAS

4 ripe bananas

200g (7oz) caster sugar

ONE 1KG (2LB 3OZ) LOAF TIN

1. Preheat the oven to 170°C (325°F), Gas 3. Grease the loaf tin with butter and dust with flour.

2. Beat together the butter and sugar in a large bowl, then peel and mash the bananas and add to the mixture. Add the beaten eggs, a little at a time, then sift in the flour and baking powder and fold into the mixture, adding the milk if it looks too dry.

3. Tip the mixture into the floured loaf tin and bake in the oven for 30 minutes or until a skewer inserted into the middle of the cake comes out clean. (Check occasionally during cooking to see if the bread browns too much. If it does, cover the tin with foil or reduce the oven temperature a little.) Remove from the oven and allow to cool slightly before removing from the tin and cooling on a wire rack. Cut into slices once cooled.

4. Next make the caramelised bananas. Place a non-stick frying pan over a medium heat and peel and cut each banana into 3. Put the sugar in a bowl and add the bananas, tossing them in the sugar, then remove the bananas from the bowl and drop them into the hot pan to allow them to caramelise. Turn the bananas during cooking to ensure they are evenly browned, then remove from the heat.

5. Top the sliced banana bread with the caramelised bananas and serve with whipped cream spooned on top.

CINNAMON-DUSTED DOUGHNUTS WITH PASSION FRUIT

These are a twist on Spanish Churros and much simpler to make than regular doughnuts, which involve a yeast dough. They need to be eaten fresh and not left around – not that I imagine they will be, as shortly after I made them for this recipe, they had all gone. Mainly on the floor, as my dog took a real shine to them. Or was it the passion fruit he liked? I think not!

SERVES 4
(MAKES 20–30 SMALL DOUGHNUTS)
VEGETARIAN

1 tbsp caster sugar
275g (10oz) plain flour, sifted, plus extra for dusting
Pinch of salt
300ml (11fl oz) boiling water
200g (7oz) caster sugar
15g (½oz) ground cinnamon
1.2 litres (2 pints) vegetable oil, for deep-frying

TO SERVE
150ml (5fl oz) double cream, whipped
4 passion fruit, cut in half

PIPING BAG WITH A 1.5CM (⅝IN) STAR-SHAPED NOZZLE

1. To make the doughnuts, place the sugar in a bowl and sift in the flour and salt. Make a well in the centre of the ingredients, pour in the boiling water and mix until well combined.

2. Place the mixture in the piping bag and pipe strips of the dough, 5–7.5cm (2–3in) long, on to a lightly floured baking sheet, then leave in the fridge for 2 hours to firm up.

3. Meanwhile, combine the sugar and cinnamon in a bowl, sprinkle on to a plate and set aside.

4. If using a deep-fat fryer, heat the vegetable oil to 180°C (350°F). Alternatively, fill a deep, heavy-based saucepan to one-third with oil and use a sugar thermometer to check that it has reached the correct temperature. (Take great care if using a saucepan: always watch over it and never fill it beyond more than a third as the hot fat may bubble up when the doughnuts are added.)

5. Remove the doughnuts from the fridge and lower them into the hot oil, in batches if necessary, cooking for 2–3 minutes or until golden brown. Remove the doughnuts from the fryer or pan and drain on kitchen paper, then transfer them on to the plate with the cinnamon sugar and roll in the mixture to coat.

6. Serve them in individual bowls with a spoonful of the whipped cream and the passion fruit squeezed over the top.

CLASSIC SPONGE CAKE

The WI are the ladies in the know when it comes to this cake, and chefs should stay out of the way. However, my Gran gave me this recipe many years ago, and I still use it to this day, so I don't think they'll mind me getting involved.

SERVES 8

VEGETARIAN

175g (6oz) butter, diced and softened, plus extra for greasing

175g (6oz) self-raising flour, plus extra for dusting

1 tsp baking powder

3 large eggs, beaten

175g (6oz) golden caster sugar

½ tsp vanilla extract

1–2 tbsp milk (optional)

3 tbsp strawberry jam

200ml (7fl oz) double cream, whipped to firm peaks

Icing sugar, sifted, for dusting

TWO 20CM (8IN) DIAMETER SANDWICH TINS WITH 4CM (1½IN) SIDES

1. Preheat the oven to 170°C (325°F), Gas 3, then lightly grease the sandwich tins with butter and dust them with flour.

2. Sift the flour and baking powder into a large bowl, then add the butter, eggs, caster sugar and vanilla extract and mix together using an electric beater until the batter is light and thick and of a dropping consistency (it will fall, but not too easily, from a spoon held above the bowl). If it seems too stiff, add a little milk to loosen the mixture.

3. Divide the mixture between the two tins, levelling the surface with the back of a spoon, and place the tins in the centre of the oven, baking for about 25 minutes or until well risen and lightly golden. To test whether the cakes are cooked, press the centre of each lightly with a finger – if the sponge springs back, it's ready.

4. Remove from the oven and allow to cool slightly, then turn out on to a wire rack. When the sponges have completely cooled, spread the jam over the base of one of the cakes, then spread the cream over the jam and place the other cake on top, dust with icing sugar and serve.

FAIRY CAKES

Fairy cakes and cupcakes have become more and more popular in recent years. The most recent wedding I went to had a tower of cupcakes as the wedding cake, and they looked and tasted great.

MAKES 24 CAKES
VEGETARIAN

100g (3½oz) butter,
diced and softened
100g (3½oz) caster sugar
2 eggs
½ vanilla pod
100g (3½oz) self-raising flour
2–4 tbsp milk (optional)
Hundreds and thousands,
to decorate

FOR THE BUTTERCREAM ICING
150g (5oz) butter,
diced and softened
150g (5oz) icing sugar, sifted
3–4 drops of food colouring

TWO 12-HOLE FAIRY-CAKE TINS

1. Preheat the oven to 180°C (350°F), Gas 4, and line the tins with paper cases.

2. Using an electric beater, cream the butter and caster sugar together in a bowl until pale and fluffy. Beat in the eggs, one at a time, then using a sharp knife scrape the seeds from the vanilla pod and add to the batter.

3. Sift the flour into the batter and carefully fold in using a large metal spoon. Add a little of the milk, if necessary, until the mixture is a soft dropping consistency (it will fall, but not easily, from a spoon held above the bowl), then half fill the paper cases with spoonfuls of the mixture.

4. Bake in the oven for 8–10 minutes or until well risen and golden brown on top and springy to the touch. Remove from the cake tins and set aside to cool on a wire rack.

5. Meanwhile, make the icing. Place the butter in a large bowl and whisk with an electric beater until light and fluffy. Then slowly add the icing sugar and keep mixing on a high speed until smooth and creamy in texture. This should take a good 5 minutes – the more you mix, the lighter the icing will be. Stir in the food colouring – dividing the icing in half, before adding the food colouring, if you want a mixture of different colours.

6. To ice the fairy cakes, swirl the icing over the cakes using a table knife, then sprinkle with hundreds and thousands to decorate.

BAKEWELL TART

This classic recipe originally came about as the result of a mistake made by a cook in a pub in Bakewell. But is the correct name Bakewell tart or Bakewell pudding? In fact, they are two different things, so I'm sticking with the tart. The most important thing is not to refrigerate it, as it causes the pastry and the filling to firm up far too much.

SERVES 8
VEGETARIAN

125g (4½oz) caster sugar

50g (2oz) ground almonds

200g (7oz) plain flour, sifted, plus extra for dusting

100g (3½oz) butter, cut into small dice, plus extra for greasing

1 large egg

Grated zest and juice of 1 lemon

Pinch of salt

Clotted cream, to serve

FOR THE FILLING
75g (3oz) butter

75g (3oz) caster sugar

Juice of 1 lemon

2 eggs

3 drops of almond extract

50g (2oz) fresh white breadcrumbs

75g (3oz) ground almonds

8 tbsp raspberry jam

25g (1oz) flaked almonds

ONE 20CM (8IN) DIAMETER LOOSE-BOTTOMED TART TIN

1. Place the sugar, almonds and flour in a food processor and mix on full speed for a few seconds. Add the butter and whizz again until just blended – the mixture should resemble fine breadcrumbs.

2. Add the egg and lemon zest, and a tiny pinch of salt. Blend again until the pastry comes together to form a ball, then wrap in cling film and place in the fridge to rest for 1 hour.

3. Grease the tart tin with butter, then remove the pastry from the fridge and place on a work surface lightly dusted with flour. Roll out the pastry and line the tin following the instructions on pages 188–9, then return to the fridge to rest for 1 hour.

4. Meanwhile, preheat the oven to 190°C (375°F), Gas 5, and make the filling. Put the butter, sugar and lemon juice in the food processor or a blender and blend until light and fluffy. With the machine running at full speed, add the eggs and almond extract and whizz until combined to a smooth paste. Then fold in the breadcrumbs and ground almonds by hand.

5. Take the pastry case from the fridge, place on a baking tray and bake blind (see page 189). Remove from the oven, then spread the jam over the bottom of the case and the almond filling over this, and return the tart to the oven for a further 20 minutes.

6. Take out of the oven, arrange the flaked almonds on top of the tart and pop it back in the oven for another 5–10 minutes or until golden brown. Remove from the oven and allow to cool, then take out of the tin, place on a plate and serve with clotted cream.

LEMON CURD TART

Being a Yorkshire man, I had to put a curd tart in my book. This is one of the all-time greats. Remember that most desserts taste so much better at room temperature and this one is no different.

SERVES 6–8
VEGETARIAN

250g (9oz) unsalted butter, softened, plus extra for greasing

125g (4½oz) caster sugar

2 large eggs, beaten

Pinch of salt

500g (1lb 2oz) plain flour, sifted, plus extra for dusting

FOR THE FILLING

100g (3½oz) caster sugar

Grated zest and juice of 3 lemons

75g (3oz) butter, diced

50g (2oz) cornflour

3 egg yolks, beaten

FOR THE VANILLA CREAM

300ml (11fl oz) double cream

100g (3½oz) caster sugar

Seeds from 1 vanilla pod

ONE 20CM (8IN) LOOSE-BOTTOMED TART TIN

1. For the pastry, cream together the butter and sugar until light and fluffy, then beat in the eggs, a little at a time. Add the salt and gradually mix in the flour until fully incorporated, then roll into a ball, cover with cling film and leave in the fridge to rest for 1 hour.

2. Meanwhile, make the filling. Place the sugar and lemon zest and juice in a heavy-based saucepan, then the add the butter and 300ml (11fl oz) of water and mix well. Place the pan over a medium heat and bring to the boil.

3. Mix the cornflour with 2 teaspoons of water and add to the lemon mixture, then bring back up to the boil and remove from the heat. Allow the mixture to cool, then whisk in the egg yolks, pass through a sieve into a bowl and set aside to cool.

4. Grease the tart tin with butter. Take the pastry from the fridge and roll out on a floured surface. Line the tin following the instructions on page 188, then return to the fridge for 1 hour.

5. Meanwhile, preheat the oven to 170°C (325°F), Gas 3. Take the pastry case out of the fridge, place on a baking tray and bake blind following the instructions on page 189. Remove from the oven and allow to cool, then spread the lemon curd filling over the base of the tart and leave to set in a cool place (but not the fridge or the pastry will harden).

6. Meanwhile, make the vanilla cream. Place the cream, sugar and vanilla seeds in a bowl and whip until light and fluffy. To serve, cut the tart into slices, and place on plates. Using a heated dessertspoon, dollop the whipped vanilla cream on to each slice.

STRAWBERRY AND ALMOND TARTS

To make these tarts really amazing, get the best-tasting strawberries you can and use all-butter puff pastry. Crank the oven high and roll the pastry nice and thin (too thick and the tarts won't cook underneath). I use marzipan but you can use crème patissière if you prefer. Serve with a scoop of vanilla or white chocolate ice cream.

MAKES 4 TARTS
VEGETARIAN

450g (1lb) ready-rolled all-butter puff pastry

Plain flour, for dusting

50g (2oz) butter, melted, plus extra for greasing

250g (9oz) marzipan

450g (1lb) strawberries

25g (1oz) flaked almonds, toasted (see method page 53)

50g (2oz) caster sugar

ONE 15CM (6IN) DIAMETER COOKIE CUTTER

1. Place the pastry on a work surface lightly dusted with flour and roll out to 3–4mm (⅛in), and prick the surface all over with a fork. Cut out 4 discs each 15cm (6in) in diameter, place on a baking sheet and leave in the fridge to rest for 1 hour.

2. Meanwhile, preheat the oven to 200°C (400°F), Gas 6, then grease a baking sheet and lightly dust with flour.

3. Roll out the marzipan to the same thickness as the pastry and cut into discs 2cm (¾in) smaller in diameter than the tarts.

4. Hull the strawberries and cut them in half, then remove the tarts from the fridge and place on the prepared baking sheet. Lightly brush the edges of the pastry with some of the melted butter and place a piece of marzipan on top of each tart. Arrange the cut strawberries on top of the marzipan, drizzle with the remaining butter and sprinkle with the sugar, then bake in the oven for 15–20 minutes or until the pastry is golden brown.

5. Scatter the toasted almonds over the top of the tarts and serve with ice cream.

CHERRY AND MACADAMIA NUT COBBLER

Some people think a cobbler is the same as a crumble but it's the top that makes them different. The UK crumble has a loose crumbly topping, as opposed to the US cobbler, which uses dough for a thicker, biscuit-like top. You can make this with almost any fruit, from apples to mulberries. Serve with double cream, ice cream or some crème fraîche.

SERVES 4–6
VEGETARIAN

1kg (2lb 3oz) cherries, pitted

25g (1oz) butter, diced

Grated zest of 1 orange

100g (3½oz) macadamia nuts, roughly chopped

75g (3oz) caster sugar

50g (2oz) sultanas

FOR THE TOPPING

275g (10oz) plain flour

2 tbsp baking powder

3 tbsp cornflour

125g (4½oz) butter, diced

3 tbsp caster sugar, plus extra for sprinkling

4 tbsp double cream

ONE 20 X 27.5CM (8 X 11IN) OVENPROOF DISH

1. To make the topping, sift the flour, baking powder and cornflour into a large bowl. Rub in the butter until the mixture is the consistency of soft breadcrumbs. Add the sugar and 3 tablespoons of the cream, roll the mixture into a ball, then wrap in cling film and leave in the fridge for 10 minutes.

2. Meanwhile, preheat the oven to 180°C (350°F), Gas 4.

3. Remove the dough from the fridge and roll into a long sausage shape about 2.5cm (1in) in diameter, then slice into discs about 5mm (¼in) thick and set aside.

4. Place a frying pan over a high heat, add the cherries and all the remaining ingredients and sauté for about 5 minutes, then tip into the ovenproof dish.

5. Arrange the cobbler topping on the top of the cherries. Brush with the remaining cream and sprinkle with sugar then bake in the oven for 20 minutes or until the pastry is golden brown.

SPICED PLUM CRUMBLE WITH CLOVE-INFUSED CUSTARD

People are often surprised at the idea of putting spices in desserts, but when you think about how commonly cinnamon and cloves are combined with apples, you realise that it does work. Anise is another spice that is lovely in homemade custard; it goes so well with traditional puddings like this. I try and grab the fresh plums from my trees before the wasps get them, but pears will also work, as will apples or peaches.

SERVES 4–6
VEGETARIAN

15 dark plums, cut in half and
stones removed

50g (2oz) butter

4 tbsp caster sugar

1 vanilla pod, split

1 star anise

Pinch of freshly grated nutmeg

1 cinnamon stick

3 tbsp golden syrup

FOR THE CRUMBLE TOPPING
150g (5oz) butter, diced and softened

150g (5oz) demerara sugar

375g (13oz) plain flour, sifted

FOR THE CUSTARD
5 egg yolks

75g (3oz) caster sugar

250ml (9fl oz) milk

250ml (9fl oz) double cream

3 cloves

ONE 20 X 25CM
(8 X 10IN) OVENPROOF DISH
WITH 2.5CM (1IN) SIDES

1. Preheat the oven to 200°C (400°F), Gas 6. Place a frying pan over a high heat, add the plums, butter and caster sugar and sauté for about 5 minutes. Add the vanilla pod, star anise, nutmeg and cinnamon stick and pour in 50ml (2fl oz) of water.

2. Add the golden syrup and bring to the boil, then reduce the heat and simmer for 6–8 minutes or until the plums break down into a thick syrup. Pour into the ovenproof dish and set aside.

3. While the plums are cooking, make the crumble topping. Place the butter and demerara sugar in a bowl and rub together until the mixture resembles breadcrumbs. Then add the flour and rub it in. Sprinkle the crumble over the plums and bake in the oven for 20 minutes or until lightly browned on top.

4. Meanwhile, make the custard. Whisk the egg yolks and caster sugar together in a bowl until well blended. Pour the milk and cream into a saucepan, add the cloves and bring to the boil.

5. Once the milk and cream are boiling, remove from the heat and pour a little on to the beaten egg yolks, stir well and pour the egg mixture into the pan. Return the pan to a low heat and, using a whisk, lightly stir to thicken the custard, but do not overheat or the eggs will scramble. As the egg yolks warm through, the mixture will thicken; keep stirring until the custard is thick enough to coat the back of the spoon. Remove from the heat and pass through a sieve, then set aside to cool.

6. Remove the crumble from the oven and allow to cool slightly before serving with the warm custard.

POACHED PEARS IN PERRY

Go to any good farmers' market and you will find a stall selling cider and Perry. Perry tastes sweeter than cider and comes mainly from three counties: Gloucestershire, Herefordshire and Worcestershire. Still made in the traditional way, the pears are crushed and pressed to release the juice, then fermented using the yeast in the skins. I wouldn't recommend substituting cider for this recipe as it just doesn't have the same taste.

SERVES 4
VEGETARIAN

1.5 litres (2½ pints) perry
175g (6oz) light soft brown sugar
Grated zest and juice of 1 lemon
Grated zest and juice of 1 orange
1 vanilla pod, split
2 cinnamon sticks
2 blades of mace
1 star anise
8 Conference pears

1. Pour the perry into a heavy-based saucepan large enough to accommodate all 4 pears standing upright. Add all the remaining ingredients except the pears and bring to the boil, then reduce the heat to a simmer.

2. Meanwhile, peel the pears, leaving the stalks intact, and cut a thin slice from the base of each fruit to enable it to stand upright in the pan. Carefully lower the pears into the pan and simmer for 45 minutes or until just tender. Take the pan off the heat and remove the pears from the liquid using a slotted spoon, placing them in a dish to cool.

3. Put the pan back on the hob and bring back up to the boil, then boil vigorously until the liquid has thickened to a syrup. Place the pears in individual bowls and pour over the syrup, serving with a scoop of vanilla ice cream. Alternatively, pour the syrup over the pears in the dish and chill for serving later.

VANILLA CURD MOUSSE WITH CHEAT'S HONEYCOMB

This is such a quick pudding that can be served as suggested, or alternatively layered up in a dish with the honeycomb on the top. Use proper vanilla pods – the flavour is so much better than essence. The best are the bourbon vanilla pods from Madagascar: thick, fat pods full of delicious, flavoursome seeds.

SERVES 6
VEGETARIAN

200g (7oz) crème fraîche
200g (7oz) curd cheese
200ml (7fl oz) double cream
Seeds from 1 vanilla pod
600g (1lb 4oz) mixed summer berries
25g (1oz) caster sugar
2 Crunchie bars

SIX 7CM (3IN) DIAMETER METAL RINGS WITH 3.5CM (1½IN) SIDES

1. Place the crème fraîche in a bowl along with the curd cheese and double cream. Add the vanilla seeds and whip until firm peaks are formed. Arrange the metal rings on a baking tray, then spoon the mixture into the rings and leave in the fridge to chill for a few hours or overnight.

2. Remove the stalks from the mixed berries and toss in a bowl with the caster sugar, then place in a pile on each plate. Remove the curd mousses from the fridge and, placing a warmed tea towel around the outside of each mould, carefully release the mousses on to each plate next to the berries.

3. Using a fine grater, grate the Crunchie bars over the top of the mousses until a small layer of chocolate honeycomb is formed, then serve.

'Being a chef: no one said it was gonna be easy, but then no one said it was gonna be this f***ing hard!'
GLYNN PURNELL

MINT CHOC CHIP ICE CREAM

Who doesn't like ice cream on a hot summer's day? I make this with plenty of fresh mint or spearmint, but if you'd prefer to add crème de menthe, reduce the sugar by 25g (1oz) or the ice cream won't set in the freezer. Serve on its own or with some hot chocolate sauce.

SERVES 4–6
VEGETARIAN

Leaves from 25g (1oz)
bunch of mint

400ml (14fl oz) milk

400ml (14fl oz) double cream

175g (6oz) caster sugar

8 egg yolks

200g (7oz) dark chocolate
(50–70% cocoa solids)

ICE-CREAM MAKER

1. First of all, finely chop half the mint leaves and set aside the remaining leaves. Pour the milk and cream into a large saucepan, add the chopped mint and heat to a simmer, then remove from the heat.

2. Meanwhile, beat the sugar and egg yolks in a bowl until pale and fluffy. Pour the milk mixture over the beaten eggs and sugar, whisking constantly as you add the milk.

3. Return the mixture to a clean saucepan and gently heat, stirring all the time, until the custard thickens enough to coat the back of the spoon. (Don't overheat the mixture or the egg yolks will scramble.) Pour through a sieve into a bowl and allow to cool.

4. When cool, roughly chop the remaining mint leaves and add to the custard, then pour into an ice-cream maker and churn until frozen. When the mixture is almost frozen, chop the chocolate into small pieces and add to the ice cream, then churn to mix in.

5. Allow to set and then serve either on its own or with some hot chocolate sauce (see page 192) poured over.

STEAMED VANILLA SUET PUDDINGS

This is one of those old-school puddings that never seem to disappoint. I don't know quite what makes it so good, perhaps it's the smell of it cooking, which reminds me of being at school and the smell wafting down the corridors while I was stuck in maths. I couldn't wait to get out of the classroom and race to the dining hall – you had to get there first else you got stuck with the dregs and skin from the custard tray, just not appetising! I tend to put golden syrup in the bottom of the basin, but you can use jam or marmalade.

MAKES 4–6 PUDDINGS

Butter, softened, for greasing

500g (1lb 2oz) self-raising flour, sifted, plus extra for dusting

250g (9oz) suet

150g (5oz) caster sugar

1 vanilla pod, split

30ml (1¼fl oz) milk

100ml (3½fl oz) golden syrup

FOUR TO SIX 5–6CM (2–2½IN) DIAMETER DARIOLE MOULDS

1. Grease the pudding moulds with the butter and dust with a little flour, then set aside.

2. Sift the flour into a large bowl, then add the suet and sugar and, using a sharp knife, scrape the seeds from the vanilla pod and add to the mixture. Then adding the milk, a little at a time, mix to achieve a dropping consistency (the mixture should fall, but not too easily, from a spoon held above the bowl).

3. Spoon a good tablespoon of the golden syrup into each of the moulds and then spoon in the cake mixture to come roughly three-quarters of the way up each mould. Cover each with a piece of foil, place in a steamer and cook for 45 minutes to 1 hour, adding more water if necessary to prevent the pan boiling dry.

4. Remove from the pan and, using a sharp knife, run around the edge of each mould to loosen. Turn out straight away on to plates and serve with some double cream or a scoop of vanilla ice cream.

COFFEE BEAN CRÈME BRÛLÉE

It's hard to travel anywhere these days without finding yet another bleeding coffee shop; along with hairdressers, they seem to be every few yards in most towns. So you don't have to go far to find good coffee beans for this recipe. Be careful not to make it too strong else it can become quite sickly.

SERVES 6
VEGETARIAN

500ml (18fl oz) milk
1 litre (1¾ pints) double cream
50g (2oz) coffee beans, freshly ground
12 egg yolks
200g (7oz) caster sugar
125g (4½oz) demerara sugar

SIX 12.5CM (5IN)
DIAMETER RAMEKINS
BLOWTORCH (OPTIONAL)

1. Preheat the oven to 130°C (250°F), Gas ½.

2. Pour the milk and cream into a saucepan and add the ground coffee, then bring to a simmer, remove from the heat and allow to cool. Place the egg yolks in a large bowl, add the caster sugar and whisk together.

3. Pour over the warm milk and the cream and whisk well, then pass through a sieve to remove any coffee grounds.

4. Ladle the mixture into the ramekins, then place on a baking sheet and bake in the oven for 1–1½ hours or until set. Remove and allow to cool.

5. Once cooled, either refrigerate or leave at room temperature. When you are ready to serve, sprinkle the dishes with the demerara sugar and caramelise using a blowtorch or by putting them briefly under a hot grill. Serve once the caramel on the top has cooled.

MELT-IN-THE-MOUTH CHOCOLATE PUDDINGS

People also call these chocolate fondants. They can be made either with a truffle centre or with sauce in the middle like this. Mine is the easier method, which I recently learnt in a 3-star restaurant in France. The most important thing is to cook the puddings for exactly the right amount of time – not enough and they will collapse when turned out, but too much and they won't be soft in the middle. Once made, they can be kept in the freezer and you can cook them from frozen when you want them.

MAKES 8 PUDDINGS
VEGETARIAN

250g (9oz) butter, softened, plus extra for greasing

225g (8oz) dark chocolate (50–70% cocoa solids), broken into pieces

8 eggs

200g (7oz) caster sugar

125g (4½oz) plain flour

EIGHT 4–5CM (1½–2IN) DIAMETER DARIOLE MOULDS WITH 6CM (2½IN) SIDES

1. Preheat the oven to 220°C (425°F), Gas 7, then grease the moulds with butter using a pastry brush and brushing in horizontal lines around insides of the tins to help the mixture rise.

2. Place the chocolate and butter into a bowl set over a saucepan of simmering water and allow to melt, then mix to a smooth consistency.

3. Meanwhile, break the eggs into a large bowl, add the sugar and whisk for 2 minutes or until pale and fluffy, then mix in the flour. Once the chocolate has melted, pour it over the eggs and sugar and stir in well.

4. Spoon the mixture into the moulds so that they are three-quarters full and give them a little tap to remove any air bubbles. (At this stage to you can freeze them if you wish but they need to defrost fully before cooking.)

5. Place on a baking tray and bake in the oven for 8 minutes only.

6. Serve them straight from the oven, turning each mould out directly on to a plate and serving with a scoop of vanilla ice cream. (A few flaked almonds under the ice cream will stop it rolling around the plate.)

BRIOCHE FRENCH TOAST WITH WARM CARAMEL APPLES

Also known as eggy bread, I love French toast for breakfast. Made with brioche like this, or alternatively with croissants, it is always delicious and can be flavoured with white chocolate or spices if you want. Serve with cream, ice cream or crème fraîche.

SERVES 4
VEGETARIAN

200g (7oz) unsliced brioche loaf
2 eggs
75ml (3fl oz) milk
25g (1oz) caster sugar
Seeds from 1 vanilla pod
40g (1½oz) butter

FOR THE CARAMEL APPLES
3 Cox apples
100g (3½oz) caster sugar
50ml (2fl oz) double cream

1. Preheat the oven to 150°C (300°F), Gas 2.

2. Cut the brioche into slices 5mm (¼in) thick, removing the crusts if you wish, then beat the eggs in a bowl, add the milk, caster sugar and vanilla seeds and mix well.

3. Melt half the butter in a non-stick frying pan over a medium heat and when the butter starts to bubble, dip the brioche in the egg mixture then place straight in the pan. Fry each slice for 2–3 minutes on each side or until browned, using the rest of the butter as you need it, then place on a baking tray and put in the oven to keep warm while you cook the apples.

4. Peel and core the apples and cut into quarters, then wipe the frying pan and place back over a high heat. Toss the apples in the caster sugar and when the pan is hot, add the apples and allow to caramelise, tossing from time to time to evenly brown. Pour in the cream, then bring to the boil to dissolve the sugar and to make a toffee sauce.

5. Place slices of brioche on to individual plates, spoon over the apples and serve with a dollop of softly whipped cream or a scoop of vanilla ice cream.

SUPPLIER LIST

FISH

Paddy's
Tim and Paddy Croft produce brilliant fresh and smoked seafood.

The Quay, Port St Mary, Isle of Man, IM9 5EF
+44(0)1624 834494
www.hookedonfish.co.uk

Fortunes Kippers Smokehouse
In my opinion, the best kippers you can buy.

Henrietta Street, Whitby, North Yorkshire, YO22 4DW
+44(0)1947 606996
http://www.fortuneskippers.co.uk

Iain R. Spink's
Iain produces original Arbroath Smokies – haddock which has been salted and smoked.

+44(0)1241 860303
www.arbroathsmokies.net

St Mawes Seafood
A fantastic quayside fish stall in the village of St Mawes, Cornwall. The fish is caught by local fisherman Pete Green.

+44(0)7792 220821
www.stmawesseafood.co.uk

The Whitstable Fish Market
South Quay, The Harbour, Whitstable, Kent, CT5 1AB
+44(0)1227 771245
www.seewhitstable.com/Whitstable-Fish-Market.html

Latimers Shellfish Deli
Delicious, fresh shellfish and other types of fish.

Shell Hill, Bents Road, Whitburn, Tyne &Wear, SR6 7NT
+44(0)191 5292200
www.latimers.com

MEAT

Colin M. Robinson
Colin is my favourite butcher. He runs two stores, selling quality lamb and other meat.

41, Main Street, Grassington, Skipton, North Yorkshire, BD23 5AA
+44(0)1756 752476
www.britnett-carver.co.uk/robinsonsbutchers/

Greenfield Pork Products
A family-run Hampshire business that sells superb free-range pork, bacon and sausages from its herd of specialist pigs.

Sunnycliff, Highbury Road, Anna Valley, Andover, Hampshire, SP11 7LU
+44(0)1264 359422
www.greenfield-pork.co.uk

Laverstoke Park Farm
An amazing, one-of-a-kind farm, selling everything from meat and vegetables to milk and cheese (the mozzarella comes highly recommended).

Overton Road, Overton, Hampshire, RG25 3DR
+44(0)800 334 5505
www.laverstokepark.co.uk

Donald Russell
An excellent Scottish butcher and meat supplier who also sells great salmon.

Harlaw Road, Inverurie, Aberdeenshire, AB51 4FR
+44(0)1467 629666
www.donaldrussell.com

Piper Farm
A family-run Devonshire farm, winner of a BBC Best Food Producer award. They rear all their own produce, which can be bought from their Exeter shop or from their website.

Cullompton, Devon, EX15 1SD
+44(0)1392 881380
www.pipersfarm.com

Broad Stripe Butchers
An online gourmet butcher with an excellent range of meat.

Fairfax Meadow, 6 Newmarket Drive, Osmaston Park Estate, Derby, DE24 8SW
+44(0)800 0911518
www.broadstripebutchers.co.uk

Vicars Game
A Berkshire-based butcher specialising in quality English meat and game.

Casey Fields Farm, Dog Lane, Ashampstead, Reading, Berkshire, RG8 8SJ
+44(0)1635 579662
www.vicarsgame.co.uk

M. Moen & Sons
A top-quality London butcher.

24, The Pavement, Clapham Common, London, SW4 0JA
+44(0)20 76221624
www.moen.co.uk

VEGETABLES

Conrad Davies' Spar
A local food hero, joint winner of the BBC Best Local Food Retailer award in 2008.

Y Maes, Pwllheli, Gwynedd, Wales, LL53 5HA
+44(0)1758 612993

Bury Market
This is one of my favourite UK markets; ideal for food lovers. It's closed on Sundays. Bury town centre

+44(0)161 2536520
www.burymarket.com

Calon Wen Organic Foods
This farmers' co-operative supplies great organic fruit and veg.

Unit 4, Spring Gardens, Whitland, Camarthenshire, SA34 0HZ
+44(0)1994 241 481
www.calonwen.co.uk

Whole Foods Market
A huge multi-storey food hall in West London. A good place to find premium and unusual produce.

The Barkers Building, 63–97, Kensington High Street, London,W8 5SE
+44(0)20 73684500
www.wholefoodsmarket.com

Fenwick
Newcastle's department store has a highly-respected food hall which promotes its local suppliers.

Northumberland Street, Newcastle upon Tyne, NE99 1AR
+44(0)191 2325100
www.fenwick.co.uk

Hampshire Farmers' Markets
With locations all over the county, these are my local markets – I highly recommend them. Check online for dates and locations.

+44(0)1420 588671
www.hampshirefarmersmarkets.co.uk

The Garlic Farm
The UK's premier grower of garlic and a source of all things garlic-related, based on the Isle of Wight.

Mersley Lane, Newchurch, Isle of Wight, PO36 0NR
+44(0)1983 865378
www.thegarlicfarm.co.uk

DELI, BAKERY & DAIRY

Valvona & Crolla
A great deli in the heart of Edinburgh.

19, Elm Row, Edinburgh, EH7 4AA
+44(0)131 5566066
www.valvonacrolla.co.uk

London Fine Foods
A great online store that supplies luxury food to top restaurants and the public.

Unit D175, New Covent Garden Market, London, SW8 5LL
+44(0)845 6439121
www.efoodies.co.uk

Neal's Yard Dairy
A highly-respected London dairy with shops in Borough Market and Covent Garden.

108, Druid Street, London, SE1 2HH
+44 (0)20 75007520
www.nealsyarddairy.co.uk

Tom's Deli
226 Westbourne Grove, Notting Hill, London, W11 2RH
+44(0)20 72218818
www.tomsdelilondon.co.uk

Cadogan and James Deli
31, The Square, Winchester, Hampshire, SO23 9EX
+44(0)1962 840805

Paul Hollywood Bread
Paul is famous in the UK for his artisan breads.

Unit 19, Miners Way Business Park, Ackholt Road, Aylesham, Kent, CT3 3AJ
+44(0)1304 841115
www.paulhollywood.com

Jeroboams
London's largest independent wine merchant – also a great place to buy artisan cheese.

7–9, Elliott's Place, London, N1 8HX
+44(0)20 7288 8850
www.jeroboams.co.uk

Mey Selections
Suppliers of high-quality farm and food products sourced from the North Scottish Highlands.

34a High Street, Wick, Caithness, KW1 4BS
+44(0)1955 606600
www.mey-selections.com

Fresh Basil
A great deli in the heart of Derbyshire.

23 Strutt Street, Belper, Derbyshire, DE56 1UN
+44(0)1773 828882

Uncle Henry's
A great farm shop to browse for meats, cheeses and veg.

Grayingham Grange Farm, Grayingham, Gainsborough, Lincolnshire, DN21 4JD
+44(0)1652 640308
www.unclehenrys.co.uk

Betty's Tea Rooms
With several locations in and around Yorkshire, you can pop in to a Betty's or shop online for delicious products.

+44(0)1423 814008
www.bettys.co.uk

INDEX

cheese: cauliflower 170
  pork burgers with rarebit 112–13
  see also individual types of cheese
cherry and macadamia nut cobbler
  206
chicken:
  baked, with artichoke purée and
    braised lentils 72
  bang bang chicken 84
  basil chicken with lime 75
  braised thighs with fennel and bay
    leaves 79
  brown stock 64–65
  Caesar salad 159
  club sandwich 66
  curry 30
  cutting into 10 pieces 62–63
  with garlic beans and chorizo
    67
  in Parmesan, almond and thyme
    crumb 69
  poached in vegetable broth 73
  roasted with sugared carrots and
    turnips 68
  spatchcock, with Greek yoghurt
    and Indian spices 71
  and wild mushroom pie 25
chicory, caramelised 51
chilli:
  and chorizo roast potatoes 168
  salt squid 41
Chinese pork and ginger dumplings
  114
chips 46
chocolate:
  chocolate, mint and satsuma
    bread 194
  melt-in-the-mouth chocolate
    puddings 215
  mint choc chip ice cream 212
  sauce 191–92
chorizo: chicken with 67
  and chilli roast potatoes 168
chutney: apple 112–13
  sweet red cabbage 81–82
clove-infused custard 208
cobbler, cherry and macadamia
  nut 206

cod steaks, tandoori 59
coffee bean crème brûlée 214
coleslaw 182
confit: honey-roast duck 83
  potato and duck confit terrine
    81–82
coriander:
  cress, mushroom soup with 16
  spiced cucumber and coriander
    salad 38
courgettes:
  courgette, tomato and basil pie
    with Dorstone cheese 22
  and shallots in black bean sauce
    143
couscous, Moroccan spiced with
  honey and almonds 123
crab with rapeseed mayonnaise and
  watercress 42
crème brûlée, coffee bean 214
croûtons: rosemary 159
  in warm duck egg salad 157
crumble, spiced plum 208
cucumber and coriander salad 38
Cullen skink 17
curd mousse, vanilla 210
curry: beef Madras 18–19
  chicken 30
custard, clove-infused 208

D

dauphinois, turnip and potato 180
doughnuts, cinnamon-dusted 198
dressing 150
  black olive and herb 43
  buttermilk 153
  honey and poppy seed 158
  mustard 94
  roast garlic 153
  see also vinaigrette
duck: honey-roast duck confit 83
  and potato confit terrine
    81–82
dumplings, Chinese pork and
  ginger 114

E

eggs: poached 136–37
  soft-boiled, with speck sandwich
    soldiers 193
  warm salad of duck egg, croûtons
    and pecorino 157
  see also omelette; soufflé
escalope of rose veal 98–99

F

fairy cakes 201
fennel:
  braised chicken thighs with 79
  braised, with breadcrumbs and
    ricotta 144
  and scallop pies 29
  trout with 53
feta:
  asparagus, feta and spinach 158
  watermelon, feta and orange salad
    with basil 160
figs, pan-fried, with mozzarella and
  mint 154
fish: filleting 32–35
  fishcakes with butter sauce 50
  proper fish and chips 46
  smoked fish pâté 36
  see also individual types of fish
fries 116

G

garlic: butter 76–78
  garlic beans and chorizo 67
  roast garlic dressing 153
gnocchi, potato: with herbs and
  saffron 126
goat's cheese:
  beetroot and shallot tartes tatin
    with 138
  courgette, tomato and basil pie
    with 22
  goat's cheese, beetroot and
    hazelnut salad 162
  leek and rocket soup with 11
  Puy lentil salad with 163